Her Life Unveiled

by

Najia Rasool

authorHOUSE®

AuthorHouse™ UK Ltd.
500 Avebury Boulevard
Central Milton Keynes, MK9 2BE
www.authorhouse.co.uk
Phone: 08001974150

First published by AuthorHouse 12/3/2008

ISBN: 978-1-4389-2632-2 (sc)

*Printed in the United States of America
Bloomington, Indiana*

This book is printed on acid-free paper.

Dedication

Bismillahi Rahmani Raheem-In the Name of Allah, the Gracious, the Merciful

I would like to dedicate this book to my father, may he rest in peace-and Yolande Naeemah Olonga, you have always been there for me, and for that, I thank you.

I would also like to dedicate this book to my sister, Bibi Zainab- for you are the glue that holds our family together.

The love for my country and its people can be best summed up with this poem by Ahmad Shah Durrani:

By blood, we are immersed in love of you.
The youth lose their heads for your sake.
I come to you and my heart finds rest.
Away from you, grief clings to my heart like a snake.
I forget the throne of Delhi
when I remember the mountain tops of my Afghan land.
If I must choose between the world and you,
I shall not hesitate to claim your barren deserts as my own

9 June 2005 (2.50 pm)

Life is always difficult whilst growing up but for me it was especially difficult as I have grown up in a country where I had never seen peace. I was born in the late 1970s when the Russians invaded my country. The Mujahadeen who were ordinary men, fought for the freedom of our country before and where now they were fighting to liberate us from the Communists. No one liked the Russians because they had invaded us and tried to change us. This was our land and in our land we could live the way we wanted to live, but with them here life was changed. What right did another country have to come and invade another, to impose their beliefs and way of life on us? This was why everyone who called themselves Afghani supported the Mujahadeen because they were Afghani and wanted to liberate us so we could live the way we knew how. We are a strong nation because although we didn't have many of the fancy weapons or big armies that other nations had we had always managed to defeat invaders like Alexander the Great, Gangez Khan, British forces. At this time my family was caught in the middle of the two, because we supported the mujahadeen as they were our people but in order to remain alive we had to appear to support the Russians. I like many others come from a big family - I have seven sisters and 4 brothers. Before the war my family was very well off as we were related to Zahr Shah Tarzi who was the King of Afghanistan. Our family house was very big so we had servants to help with the cleaning and daily up keep of the property. Within our compound we had our own Mosque which was used by the whole family and we also had a couple of four bedroom apartments that we rented out. Our back garden was so big that dad had to employ just one person whose job was just to look after it. We had orchards filled with fruit trees from plums, peach to grapes, figs and pomegranates. During summer the garden was full of flowers of all colours especially roses as they were mum's favourite. I still remember the hot summer evenings when the garden servants would wash the garden and lay out our beds so that we could relax and enjoy the warm nights outside. Dad even had someone to drive him to work. Life was so good!

Imagine being the youngest child but instead of getting all the attention you feel like you are the ugly duckling – well welcome to my life. My older sister Elida who I come after was very pretty and everyone always gave her all the attention. She was always given the best shoes, clothes, and allowed to got out with her friends but I was never given that chance. Mum always made me do the house work and when she did the smallest of things my parents would praise her. She looked so much like my dad and hence they were very close. Once I was left alone with my 2 older sisters as my mum had to go to Pakistan to see my older brother Ali, and Elida would use the opportunity to slap me and pull my hair. Samir was the oldest out of the three of us and she loved me so much. As mum had to go to Pakistan frequently Elida would wake me up very early and make me sweep in the garden in order to do all the house work. At my tender age of six I looked forward to finally getting away from Elida and starting school as I would be surrounded by other children and maybe I could have a 'normal childhood'. The first couple of months were very exciting and I made many new friends and things looked bright but then one dark day a stray missile landed in our classroom. There was blood everywhere, screaming children, and total chaos and I was gripped with fear. With no where to run all I could do was just stand against the wall and pray that we would get out alive. After a few minutes brave men broke down the door and took us all to safety. Many people told me that I was one of the lucky survivors but I didn't feel like that because I had lost my first best friend to that accident. We had not only shared the same name but we had shared many memories and now all those were dead, just like her. For as long as I can remember I had always been afraid as here I was, this 6 year old that has seen her best friend dying. Every time I heard gunshots I would run and pick up my jumper then hide in the cupboard spending hours on end waiting. I'm not to sure what I was waiting for – the war to come to an end or maybe perhaps to wake up from this bad dream. After spending time trying to find me mum would open the cupboard I would yell at her not to open the door as the light was coming in. Everyone thought I was crazy but that didn't bother me because all I knew was that hiding here made me feel safe. When Samir got married and left the country to go live with her husband I felt so alone and sad. She had looked after me and I felt safer when she was around.

One evening when mum was home a stray missile damaged our house and mum was injured and went into a comma for 6 months. After six months mum was still not recovering and had to be taken to Islamabad in Pakistan to receive treatment. I was left at home with Elida when another stray missile hit our house. It caused a fire and the entire house was engulfed in flames. I was terrified and gripped with fear. Was this to be my last day I kept thinking? We managed to break the window and escape, but only away from the fire. There we were standing in front of what we called home which had now been burnt to the ground, all alone in the cold. We had nothing as everything had been destroyed by the fire and we were alone as everyone had moved from the area because of the war. We struggled to find something to eat, the nights were cold and we were just two scared children wishing for someone to take us to safety.

We decided to travel about two hours away where we stayed with a family who used to work for my family. They were very kind and took us in until my dad returned from Pakistan. On his return we knew that we couldn't return to our old house as it was no more so we began building a small house of our own. Mum was still in Pakistan, although she had recovered from her comma she still required regular treatment for the injuries she received from the missile attack. Life was hard as we had no money, no food and no home. Why did life have to be so unfair? After spending long hours working, we finally finished this basic shelter that we would call home for now. Mum was much better now and came home much to my relief, and although things were still very bad, at least we still had each other. After some time Elida got married and left and even though

I felt she was always the favoured child I knew I would miss her. The man who had taken us in became very ill and needed medical treatment, but we had no money. Quickly my dad borrowed some money from someone in order to buy him some medicine but it was too late. There lay his lifeless body in a wheelbarrow that had been used to transport this sick man to the basic clinic. How could this happen to such a good man? My family and I mourned for the next few months as this man was like part of our family.

A couple of months went by and we increasingly knew that we had to leave the country in order to have a chance of a better life. It was then decided that mum and I would go to Pakistan where my older brother Ali and his family were staying. Our journey was through Balduck passage which was long, uncomfortable and complicated as it involved bribing many policemen at check points which had become a common site. For many miles we would have to walk until our feet ached and bleed because our shoes had been worn out by this long tedious journey, but we knew we had to carry on. Once over the border in Pakistan we came to a small town called Chaman were we had to get up at four in the morning to catch a bus which would take us down the Qhoja Mountains to Quetta. On the eve of our journey to Quetta there was news of two trucks that had collided on the narrow ridged road because many buses and trucks don't have lights when driving at night. Many innocent people died because the accident happened in an area far from any city and most drivers were too scared to help because they would be asked too many questions about the immigrants they were carrying. The only way the families of the dead would find out of their loved ones fate was if someone came to report the accident at the destination police station, then the police would inform families.

When we got to Quetta we had to wait in the cold until we finally got a lift from a man with a horse drawn cart who then took us to Ali's house which was just outside Quetta. We had just about made it! I say 'just about' because when we arrived we were tired, soaking wet, cold, with painful bleeding feet tired from the long walk we had endured – but we had made it! I was relieved and thankful that at last we were safe. Things always look so simple in a child's eyes and I guess that's how I saw everything too. The next couple of days I recovered from the long journey which had left me with a high fever. As we had no money to buy medicine so my cousins gave me herbal medicine and within a couple of days I was well enough.

We lived with them for some time not knowing what had happened to dad. Then one day he arrived but he was badly injured as he had been hit by a bus which left his leg badly bruised. One of my uncles came and took dad to the hospital and he had to have an operation because he had broken the bone and the wound had an infection. However we could not afford the operation so once again mum used herbal medicine to help him get better. Even though dad was in pain he didn't say anything but even as a child I could see it in his eyes and this made me feel upset because there was nothing I could do to help him.

On top of all this we were no longer welcome in Ali's house as his wife wanted us to move out. I felt sad and hurt but at the same time I also felt angry as family is supposed to be there for each other always and here we were being evicted from Ali's house. Ali's wife didn't really like us even though we had always given her everything she needed. She had come from a poor family that dad always helped and her father asked if Ali would marry her which he did. All those childhood memories of how dad never wanted to see anyone suffering all came back to haunt me – did she not remember this? This was when I realise that life is never fair, you can give people your heart and do so much for them but when things change and you need their help some people will turn a blind eye and forget all you did for them. I wanted to scream and remind her and Ali that we were family, remind them that we needed them that I needed them but I couldn't. I just stood there, lost for words with the colour drained from my face, feeling as though my world had just crashed down all around me.

We were given an ultimatum, either we leave or she leaves. How could she speak to us like this? How could she disrespect us like this? Dad tried to reach an agreement with them that we would leave in the morning but they weren't having it. Minutes later the door bell rang and it was a mini-bus that they had hired to carry their belongings and them away. Oh Mashallah, was this the same young lady who we had helped and loved so many years ago? We later discovered that they had planned this whole fiasco because her mother was coming to visit them from America. She had rented out another house with her sister so she could move in after fighting with us. After about two weeks Ali came over and told us we had to leave because he wanted to rent this property out and so mum saw no other way but to move back to Kandahar. She then went to phone my brother Yousef in Germany just to inform him that we would be going back and to say good-bye. Yousef pleaded with mum to change her mind because he would rent out a place for us in Quetta and that everything would be okay. Mum went to Quetta where she found an apartment that was suitable for us to rent out whilst dad and I stayed in Ali's house. It wasn't long until she found a place and we then joined her. My sister in America, Yasmeen sent us some money to buy household furniture and this became our home for a while. I was happy because now at least I was with my parents the people who had always tried to make life better for me. Being here with them was all I needed. Maybe now life would be normal even though I was still not in school I didn't mind. I learnt a lot at home like how to speak Urdu by watching television. I made friends with my neighbour who then helped me by teaching me how to write. One day I went over to their house and I was invited in and her daughter came screaming in. She was cold and wanted the heating on because it was free anyway as they were tapping into our source. I was surprised that these people could take advantage of us, but I remained silent until the bill came. My parents were surprised that the bill was so high and then I felt it would be unfair of me to keep my parents in the dark of what was really going on. Dad met her husband at the local Mosque and told him about the high bill we had received but did not confront him with what he knew but he remained silent about his misdemeanours. On the way home they met another friend who was an electrical engineer and dad explained about the bill. Dad asked the engineer to have a look at the wires in our house and in our neighbour's house and immediately our neighbour refused. The engineer told him he could not refuse, and then they went to his house and checked the wires and found that they were connected to our electricity wires. Our neighbour denied knowing anything about this.

We didn't really keep in touch with Ali because although he was one of us he had hurt us. However his son Amir, who was younger than me had a special bond with dad and couldn't keep away. As young as he was he would save up every Rupee he got his hands on in order to come and visit. We really wanted to see him but not if his father didn't approve which was the case. Unfortunately Amir told his older brother who went and spilt the beans to Ali probably to get more attention and Ali was furious. He beat Amir until this poor little boy had to be taken to hospital. Were we so bad that he would beat a child so badly in order to stop him from seeing us? Poor little Amir, all he wanted was to see us. What was so wrong with that? Dad was upset, mum was in tears and I just couldn't believe it! I couldn't help feeling like everywhere we went things never went right for us and I couldn't understand why. We were good people who always helped others regardless, so what happened to the saying 'one good turn deserves another!'

Well later on that year we got some news from my sister Zainab who had moved to London many years ago after she got married. She wanted to sponsor us to come over to London and arranged for us to go to the Embassy in Quetta for some interviews. We had a couple of interviews there over the next couple of weeks. These were long interviews at the British

Embassy and often we had to wait long periods of time just to be interviewed. We were interviewed by an English man who was not very polite and often we felt like he was looking down upon us. He would sit there at his desk with his feet on the desk, very relaxed asking us questions. Of course in many cultures this is seen as very rude. We had an interpreter present who would translate everything the man said for us into Pashto just to ensure that we didn't miss anything. Some days we were seen very quickly and we would return home early whilst other days we would spend the whole day waiting to be seen. The receptionist would tell us that our interviewer was not in but on several occasions you would see him walking around the offices and wonder why they had to lie to us. Why did they have to treat us like this, disrespect my parents for what? I hoped that the people in London were not going to be like the people here. Very often westerners called my people and many others uncivilised but this is exactly what I saw when I looked at them. Finally we got clearance to go to Karachi which was a bigger embassy in order to get the last interviews done to get our pass to London.

Karachi is a distance from Quetta and an even greater distance when you are still a young girl. I was excited and my heart couldn't stop beating fast. I felt like screaming with joy as my mind raced out of control thinking about possible new life prospects ahead. What was London like? It had to be better than this, surely. Perhaps all that waiting had paid off and we were beginning to get a streak of good luck. How I wanted the streak to continue for life because looking at what my family and I had been through – did we not deserve to be happy? The bus journey was uncomfortable and ten hours long as the bus was old and allowed the cold to come in. There were many people in the bus as the drivers didn't stick to the correct carrying capacity of the bus but it was more like -'get in as many as you can.' Apart from the bad smell of smoke produced by the shisha pipe that the driver was smoking, many people were sweating and that filled the air with a pungent smell that made my stomach turn. We occasionally stopped much to my relief as I could get some fresh air, as well as something to eat and drink. The bus would stop at places that were dimly lit by paraffin lanterns that hung from wooden stall that sold water and fruits. There were no toilets so we would have to go behind a couple of bushes to relieve ourselves which I couldn't stand, so as a result I didn't drink a lot of water. The driver would replenish his shisha pipe which helped him remain awake during this long journey because many of these drivers only get about 4 hours sleep as they had to drive back and forth in order to make a living. The bus broke down once or twice as we neared Karachi but the bus driver knew what the problem was and fixed it. It was probably a reoccurring problem as this bus was old and on its last journeys but the bus driver would not let it go until he had ensured that he had squeezed every last bit of power from it. Eventually we got to Karachi and it felt good to walk around freely as I had been sitting on mum's lap for much of the journey and I couldn't feel my legs. As the blood re-circulated around my legs I wondered how many more of these journeys we would have to make. We stayed with some relatives whilst we were there. They were not well off; hence they lived in a scrawny 2 bedroom flat in a deprived part of Karachi. Even though I was drugged with sleep as I was tired from the long uncomfortable journey I walked straight not wanting to touch the dirty walls that held this dilapidated structure that was home to so many people. Their flat was very small and I couldn't believe that 10 people slept in the two bedrooms. Oh my where were we going to sleep? Was there room for three more? I had often heard stories about how two families with five of more children would share small rooms like the one right before my eyes but always dismissed it as just being exaggerated stories but right in front of my eyes was a similar situation. Although it was just one family it was the same thing because there was no privacy for anyone. Anyway to my surprise we were welcome and I slept in between my parents and I slept like a baby probably because I was tired from the long journey or perhaps because I felt safe sleeping here hundreds of miles away from home that was being bombed by the Russians. In the morning I was woken up early in order to get ready to go to our appointment with the British Embassy.

We arrived at the embassy where we had to wait a while for the interviewer to come and get us. As we waited my attention was diverted to the receptionist who looked very busy answering the telephone and writing down messages. I soon got bored and then diverted my attention to the man who was watering the plants in the courtyard. Finally the receptionist called out our name as it was our turn. We went into the interview room where an interpreter was present as well as our interviewer who introduced himself as Mr Smith. He was a tall middle-aged man with dark hair, blue eyes and coffee stained teeth. He wore a light blue shirt which had the top buttons unbuttoned because of the heat and black trousers with shiny black shoes. We sat down and the interview began. Mum and dad were asked many questions which were translated by the interpreter and they answered each one of them. I sat there and watched Mr Smith who kept writing down everything my parents said. He appeared understanding occasionally nodding his head. At last the interview came to an end and we were told to come back the following day for another one. Although I was bored during these interviews I preferred to be here with my parents than left with my cousins in their small flat.

For the next couple of days this became routine, we would go to the embassy wait and be seen and other days wait only to be told to come tomorrow! The interviews were not always the same, some days they would simply just interview my parents other days I was asked some questions. I was a very shy child always kept to myself probably because I had taken to heart how people had judged me, so I always protected myself by almost becoming invisible. Since the age of nine I had always worn a scarf that covered my complete face just leaving a narrow slit for my eyes. This was my hiding place from the judging outside world, where I felt protected. During a couple of interviews Mr Smith would ask to just interview me. I could always see the worry on my parents faces when I would stand up and be led into the interview room. I could feel my knees shaking and my heart pounding so loud I was worried that he could also hear it. The interpreter was also present at these interviews which at least made me feel better because he spoke Pashto. I was asked to remove my scarf and this sent cold shivers down my spine as this was my amour to protect me against the 'evil world'. I was scared because I had never shown my face to a complete stranger and here I was getting ready to take off my scarf for this stranger who was a man. My parents were strict and I was worried how I would explain to them what had happened. How would they react? All of these questions buzzed in my head until I was brought back from my day-dream by Mr Smith who was asking me if I was alright. I knew I had to do this so without wasting any more time I took my scarf off and sat there gazing at the floor because I wasn't supposed to look at this stranger in the eyes according to my culture. Mr Smith watched me carefully as I answered the questions probably to try and read whether I was telling the truth. The interview began with simple questions like – What is your name. The questions became more difficult and I answered them to my best knowledge. One question that almost made me laugh was– are these your real parents? Of course they were my real parents I thought. Before I gave my answer I was told that I should be completely honest because if I tried to mislead them they would find out and I would be returned immediately. This didn't really scare me because I had told the truth about everything. The more personal interviews I had with Mr Smith the more confident I became and gradually I began to look him straight in the eye. I wanted him to see that I was not scared of him or the questions he had posed at me. Finally we were told that this session of interviews had been completed and that we should go home and wait to be called back in a couple of months. So we returned to our home in Quetta the same way we had arrived here – by bus. I was pleased that we had finally finished this part of the interview and we could now go home.

Although the bus journey is long I sleep probably because my little body was tired from all this. I fell into a deep sleep and dreamt about my home back in Kandahar and how beautiful it was then, this serine environment totally disappearing leaving just smoky ruins. My heart felt heavy and I wanted to scream but I can't then I suddenly woke up and felt the cold sweat droplet running down my face. Thank God it is just a dream; I was safe sitting here between my parents. I began to think about some of my cousins who weren't as lucky as I was, they were still at home suffering and there was nothing I could about it but pray.

I quickly got back to my usual daily routine of getting up early to do the house work and help make breakfast for dad. Everyone got on with their lives as we eagerly waited for the day when we would receive a letter from the embassy to tell us when our next appointment would be. I gradually forgot about it. I would pass my time by reading the Quran and saying my prayers five times a day. After about two months dad decided to call the embassy as we had not heard anything from them about our next appointment. They told him that Mr Smith was no longer interviewing us and that the interview was currently in Britain and we would receive a letter about our next interview soon. A couple of weeks went by and still we heard nothing until one day we received a letter in an official brown envelope. It was addressed to dad and had the embassy stamp on it. He quickly ripped the envelope opened and silently read it and sighed. I stood there and I felt like my heart stopped beating. I had mixed emotions, half of me was excited and the other half was scared. What was written in the letter? I wanted to yell at dad to hurry up and read it out loud so my curiosity could be killed and then I would know what happens next. The next thing dad announces that we need to go back to Karachi for another set of interviews.

So we had to make our way back to Karachi using the same means. When we got there, we had to wait in a long queue in the scorching sun as it was mid-summer. The queue moved along very slowly and unfortunately by the time our turn came the Embassy closed so we had to come back the following day. Once again we stayed with our relatives in their 2 bedroom flat. We had to get up early the next morning to get to the Embassy early in order to secure a place in the queue. Once the embassy doors opened at 9 in the morning we waited to be seen to. Once our turn came we were told that the interviewer Mr Williams was about to leave as he only worked from 9 to 12 and that we shouldn't come back tomorrow as he was away for a week on business in Islamabad. This was annoying as we had arranged that we would only be in Karachi for a week now it seemed it would be a lot longer. After a week we returned only to be told that he was off-sick and that we should check if he is in after a few days. Dad continued to call everyday to find out if he was back, but only to be told no. When he finally came back to work we were unable to get an appointment because he had to deal with the back-log. Our case was passed on to someone else and we would ring and be told to ring after 2 hours. Finally after 2 hours we would call and the receptionist would tell us that our interviewer was out for lunch or busy. After many attempts we finally we given an appointment which was supposed to be after 5 days. We attended our interview which lasted a couple of hours and when that was over we were told to return in the morning. We returned very early at around 7 and once again we had to wait. I was tired of waiting and just wanted to go home as it was hot. I wanted to sit in the shade and drink ice cold water but this would just have to remain a dream as there was not a tree in site on the streets of Karachi. The sun continued to scorch down upon us with no mercy and I became irritated. I wanted to ask mum how long we would have to wait, but I knew that she too was hot, tired and didn't know the answer to my question. We waited about 4 hours but this felt like forever. The receptionist finally told us that we have to wait till 5.30 to see the interviewer. So we waited and I passed the time by staring at the people passing by and my mind raced by thinking about what was going to happen once we had this interview. Would we have to come back here tomorrow? So all we could do was wait, and so we did. Finally we were called to come into the office where a gentleman told us that he had made numerous calls to London and other places and that it had all paid off because he was going to issue us with our visas. I was relieved and felt like a huge weight had been lifted off my tiny shoulders. He would send us a letter in the post informing us where to pick up our tickets for our flight to London. We would have to return to Quetta because that was where the letter would be sent and I hoped that this time we would get the letter promptly. He also informed us that the visas were only valid for six weeks so we had to move fast in order to ensure our travel. I was excited and wanted to jump for joy because finally the waiting had paid off and the gentleman was giving us some good news. There was part of me that hoped that this was genuine and not 'tararf' – a white lie. Mum and dad were very surprised and I guess reserved, because they didn't want to show their excitement just in case it was not meant to be.

We went back to our relative's house where we spent the night and got ready for the long journey ahead of us back to Quetta. Our relatives asked us how our interview went but we didn't tell them of the latest developments. Dad just tells them that we are going home and that the embassy would send us a letter informing us of when our next interview was. That night I couldn't sleep as I was excited about everything, but I knew I had to rest because the next day was going to be tiresome. We had to make a very early start in order to be at the bus station by 5 in the morning as the buses often got full quickly. The bus that we took seemed better than the one we used the very first time we came to Karachi or perhaps it seemed so because I had now always learnt never to expect too much, so it seemed better. Although the journey was long and the sun was blazing down on us I was happy. I sat next to mum the whole journey and would occasionally drift into sleep until I was woken up by these rude young boys who kept pulling my hair. They thought it was funny but I didn't. However I was not going to let them ruin my good mood so I just ignored them. I continue thinking about my life ahead of me. Half of me is scared but the other half just couldn't wait, wait to start again, and wait to live a normal happy life if anything like that existed!

As the bus comes to a stop at the station I realise that our journey has finally come to an end. Now we can go home and begin our preparations for our new life far away from here. When we finally get home and I see my brother Faroqe and I want to run and tell him the good news, but then I remember that I was sworn to secrecy by mum and dad. I am happy to see him so I don't say a word about the events in Karachi and just tell him that I was happy to be home. Suddenly behind him emerges a small child who resembles Ali's child. After carefully examining this child I realise it is Ali's first child and then I am puzzled. What is he doing here? Ali and his wife appear from inside the house and greet us with open arms. I can't believe it. Why are they here? Why are they being so nice to us? Are these the same people who were ready to disown us a couple of years ago. I could read the look on dad face that he was not pleased. Everyone goes inside to talk and I go to my room where I can hear what is being said by everyone in the lounge. I wanted to know what they were doing here. From gathering bits and pieces of the story it appeared that they had fallen out with Ali's sister-in-law who had thrown them out. With no where to go and no money they found they way to our house. Faroqe was at home alone when they arrived very late at night and he only let them in because he felt sorry for the children who were feeling cold. I was upset and hoped dad would remind them about how they had treated us and what they had put us through. I didn't want them to be here. When we needed them they didn't want to know so I felt like they were using us and I wanted to tell them how I felt. Why was dad being so patient with them? I didn't hear them leaving and I was confused- why had dad not told them to leave? After thinking about it I came to the conclusion that dad was worried about the children. This was his weakness, because he couldn't tell them to leave because he would be punishing the innocent children. Ali and his family stayed with us for a week and during this time we had to start preparing for our journey. We had so much to do but how could we when we felt like prisoner in our own home. We continued to keep our secret and slowly mum began to pack certain things away. I was anxious about how long the letter would take to arrive, so every time I would hear a bicycle bell ring I would run to the door quickly a peep through a small crack to see if it was the postman. This became a routine until one day I saw the him walking towards our door. I wanted to yell to mum to come quick but then I realised she would wonder how I knew he was coming to the door so I quickly went to my room. The postman knocked on the door and mum went to open the door and receive the letter. She didn't say anything to me or anyone. I knew it had to be the letter we had been waiting for. I acted like I knew nothing but deep inside I was excited.

Mum didn't say anything to me about the letter and after ten days I was told that we were going into town to run an errand. I got ready and we left together with dad. On the way there mum told me about the letter and I tried to act surprised and once again I was sworn to secrecy. I was also told that we were going to pick up our tickets from a travel agents office. I was excited but didn't show it as I had now become a master at hiding my emotions. The travel agents office was a small house and as we walked towards the door I couldn't help but notice how beautiful the area was. The door was ajar and once we walked in I felt a cool breeze blowing through my scarf. It was clean and had pictures of beautiful resorts that I didn't even know existed when and a short, fat gentleman dressed in shalwa kameez came to greet us. He had arranged our tickets and he spoke to dad about the arrangements. We then had to wait and we didn't mind as we had grown accustomed to this. We were then interviewed separate starting with dad then mum and finally myself. The interview took about 30 minutes for each person and during the interview the gentleman was making phone calls and discussing the arrangements with us. When it came to my turn I was scared because I didn't know what this was about and what he was going to ask me. He asked me basic questions like they did at the embassy then he gave me instructions about our journey. We were each given a white bag with the letters PIA written in green on the side. We were told that we each had to hold these bags in order to be identified by the people meeting us up in Karachi. This whole process of obtaining our tickets took approximately two hours.

When we got home we had to act like we had just been on an ordinary trip to town. That night I couldn't sleep because my imagination was racing wild. I wanted to tell the whole world about my journey but I couldn't. So there I was tossing and turning trying to answer all the questions I had. Next morning I got up early at the sound of the Azzan and as I got ready for prayers my heart was filled with joy. I said my prayers making sure to thank Allah for the goodness and kindness he had shown us. I also prayed that we would be able to travel there safely. I was happy that everything was well on its way. Mum and dad continued to slowly pack things away but still remained silent about our mission. A week later dad's younger brother came to visit and dad broke the news to him. He couldn't believe it and he cried loud as he didn't want us to go. I thought that he was being silly – where was he when we needed him? I hoped dad would not change his mind just because his brother all of a sudden showed his emotions. When he left dad sat down with mum and told her that he couldn't leave. Mum was upset and told him that he had to come as this was our only chance to make a better life. Many people would die for this chance and here he was just about to throw it away. I was very upset with dad. How could his brother have so much control over him? I buried my face in my pillow and cried myself to sleep wishing that I would wake up from this bad dream. Next day we sat as a family mum and dad talked about my dad's decision. Mum persuaded him to come with us then stay for a while after which he could come back. I sat there staring at the floor in silence not wanting to make eye contact with either mum or dad as I was on the point of tears. After a few days dad changed his mind I guess because he looked at me and knew that he couldn't leave me to grow up without him being around. I was happy and hoped that he wouldn't change his mind again.

With only one and a half weeks left until our departure I noticed that mum and dad were packing more and more stuff away. Slowly the house I had come to know as home began to look less and less like home as they began packing away things. We would get relatives coming to see us because uncle had told everyone that we were leaving. They all wanted to stay and see us off the day of our departure so all the rooms of our house were full and so others would have to go to my cousin's house which was close by to sleep there as we had no more room. The night before our flight to Karachi I couldn't sleep, not only because I was so excited but because my cousins were all there and we were talking and laughing. This was the happiest I had been in a long time and it felt good. The next day I couldn't wait for the time to pass until we had to go. Finally we began to get ready and I wore nice yellow shalwar kameez that mum had bought for me. All our bags were put outside and when the cars came to pick us up all our relatives started to cry. Emotions came over me as I saw everyone crying including mum and dad and I too couldn't stop the tears that I had tried so hard to suppress run down my rosy cheeks. For a moment I felt I couldn't go but then reality hit me and I realised that this was the one chance and I had to take it. When we got to the airport we checked in our luggage but kept our hand luggage which was the small white bags we had been instructed to always hold then we said our last good-byes then we had to go up many stairs in order to get to the departure lounge. We sat and waited in the lounge which was surrounded by glass so we could see the 2 PIA aircraft parked at the departure gate. As I looked out I could see the blazing heat rising off the tarmac making the background look hazy. The departure lounge was relatively full of other passengers who were all shouting trying to speak over all the noise. I sat there quietly observing my surroundings thinking about my friends that I had left behind. Although it had only been about an hour or two since I was with them this felt like eternity to me and I didn't know how I would survive without them. I felt alone even though I was with mum and dad. After a short while an announcement was put out for us to proceed to the boarding gate. We had to go down stairs and walk to the aircraft which was parked far away. It took us about 20-30 minutes to get to the aircraft because mum and dad walked slowly. I was kind of glad that they did because my little legs got tired and by the time I got to the aircraft I was out of breath.

Once we got to the aircraft we found our seats and waited for the aircraft to depart. The cabin was clean and the cabin crew team which comprised of ladies and gentlemen who were smartly dressed. The ladies wore green shalwar kameez and a scarf that was worn in a fashionable way. They were all wearing make-up and were very beautiful and the gentlemen were very well groomed. As I looked around the cabin I noticed that the majority of the passengers were men, all of which were smartly dresses, I guess they were businessmen on business trips. I turn around to look at mum and dad who are busy talking but I couldn't make out what about. From what I could hear it seemed dad had decided that he wanted to go back and mum is trying to persuade him to stay by telling him that he has come this far he may as well continue the journey. She finally persuaded him to stay and then got up to go and talk to the cabin crew. When she returns she informs us that we are moving to a window seat which makes me smile because I loved looking down at how small everything looked from way up there. I let dad sit by the window, anything to keep him from changing his mind and I knew that I could still look out if I wanted to. The cabin crew made a couple of announcements, and closed the doors, then demonstrate the safety procedures to us. We then felt the aircraft being pushed back and we heard the engines being turned on. This wasn't a very big aircraft but I could feel the power coming from the two engines that were hanging from the wings. Slowly we taxied towards the runway and the cabin lights are dimmed and the last announcements are put out. When we got to the runway the pilot brought the aircraft to a complete stop and increased the power of the engines which now felt like they are going to take the wings with them. We finally started to inch forward then we gained speed and as I gaze outside I couldn't focus on anything because the aircraft was moving too fast. The front wheel lifted off the ground and then I felt a little scared. I felt like reaching out to hold mum and dad's hand but I can't, I just sat there and held on to my seat. We continued to climb and twenty minutes into the flight the seat belt sign went off and the cabin crew began to serve drinks and light snacks. We each ordered tango which was served in a plastic cup and a soggy sandwich that had one slice of tomato and cucumber and loads of onions. This put me off as I didn't like the idea of having onion breath, and although I was hungry as I didn't get a chance to eat when I was at home I decided not to eat. Mum and dad also didn't eat the sandwiches and continued to talk about what was going to happen to us next. I sat quietly listening in on the conversation but acting like I wasn't and secretly hoping dad wouldn't change his mind again. I also kept praying that we would be safe and that he wouldn't leave us. The cabin crew did a last inspection of the cabin collecting all the dirty cups and rubbish from the passengers. We were told to fasten our seat belts and get ready for landing. I could see everything on the ground getting bigger as we descended and I pinched myself because I thought I was dreaming. Was I really on the way to London? Was my dream finally coming true? The landing was a little bumpy but I guess I didn't really notice as I was day-dreaming about London. Before I knew it we had disembarked and were in Karachi Airport terminal building waiting for our other luggage.

Dad ensured we had all our belongings and we made our way out of the baggage hall. The airport was huge with different types of passengers waiting for connecting flights. There were many different aircraft outside, some big and others small. The airport was very clean and there were many shops filled with jewellery and clothes. We were all looking around as there was so much to see as we passed through the terminal. Dad reminded us to each hold the white bags that the travel agent had given us because this was how the people meeting us would identify us. As we walked towards the doors leading outside the terminal we saw the crowds of anxious relatives waiting for their loved ones to appear. Once we step outside we were hit by the heat and the noise from the crowd. I looked around and saw people hugging family members they hadn't seen for a while. There was a woman hugging her son who had come back after so long and she was crying tears of joy. I could see children screaming and others greeting their loved ones 'Salaam Alekuim!' I continued walking behind my parents who weren't too sure who they were supposed to be looking for until two gentlemen approached dad. They are both tall, with neatly cut moustaches that reminded me of pastry brushes! They wore white shalwar kameez with black waistcoats. They took us to the hotel we were going to be staying. It was a big, beautiful five-star hotel that had a beautiful reception area. To get to our apartment you had to go through the reception and out into the garden as it was on the ground floor. There were many flowers around the garden and it brought back memories of my home in

Kandahar. Our apartment had two bedrooms and each had its own bathroom. The apartment had double doors leading onto the porch that was surrounded by flowers. We were all tired from our journey so we each took a shower and changed our clothes and had tea. I sat on the porch and admired my surroundings and enjoyed my cup of tea. I hadn't eaten all day and my stomach was now making noise. There was a knock at the door and when dad opened it in came one of the men who had brought us from the airport. He told us to come with him as we were going to have dinner. He took us to the roof where they had a buffet in the middle of the room. The waitresses were smartly dressed in black trousers and white shirts and ties. I could smell lamb kebabs cooking in the kitchen and my salivary glands began to water. We sat down and ordered salad and lamb kebabs that were being cooked right in front of us. The buffet was full of food and I saw everything from biriyani to fruits and salads. The food was delicious and I directed all my attention to my plate. This was perfect I thought and I continued letting my taste buds explore all these different tastes. As the sun set a cool breeze rustled the flowers that where set around the restaurant and there was a relaxed atmosphere. I was tired and wanted to fall asleep right there but I tried to keep my eyes opened because everything was so beautiful and I wanted the moment to last forever. We return to our room to rest because we knew that we had another long day ahead of us. As I lay on my bed I couldn't close my eyes because I was anxious for morning to come. At the back of my head I knew that I need the sleep but I couldn't get to sleep, so I just closed my eyes and rested. I drifted in and out of sleep and some-times I would get up and look around not knowing where I was.

Early the next morning at about 4 there was a knock at our door. Dad got up and opened it and a man told him that it was time to get up as our transport was going to be here to pick us up in about half an hour to take us to the airport. My eyes were heavy but I got up and took a quick shower and changed into a new set of clothes. Half an hour later there was another knock and it was the man who had brought us here. He took our luggage and led us to the car which was waiting outside. As we drove towards the airport the streets were empty and most of the lights in the houses were turned off. The journey was short and when we got to the airport the man helped us with our luggage. All our luggage was checked in and he took us to the departure lounge. He then waited there with us and made small chat with mum and dad. I sat there and looked around at the other passengers in the departure lounge. There were many different types of people there from Arabs in their long white flowing robes to Easterns (Westeners) who were dressed in tight shorts and t-shirts. Apart from their looks you could easily pick them out of a crowd because of the way they dressed because no one from Asia or even the Middle East would wear those clothes. This was because of our culture differences- I guess where East meets west. There were many different languages spoken in that departure lounge from English to Arabic. I was memorised by the diversity of the cultures within that departure lounge.

Finally it was time to board and the man led us to our departure gate and I hoped that we wouldn't have to walk a long distance to the aircraft like how we did in Quetta. The man instructed us to go through the doors and get onto the bus which would take us to the aircraft. I was relieved because although it was still early and cool I didn't really feel like walking to the aircraft carrying my bag. We thanked the man and said good-bye to him and went to board the bus. Once we got to the aircraft we found our seats and got ready for our long journey. I was tired and my eyes began to get heavy. I wanted all the passengers to hurry up and take their seats so that we could begin our journey. I was worried that dad would once again decide to change his mind so I wanted the doors to close so we could take off as soon as possible before the thought even crossed his mind.

This aircraft was massive compared to the one we had travelled on from Quetta and had 2 huge engines that hung from each wing like giant pendulums. The aircraft glistened in the morning sun making the colours of PIA look lovely. I sat back in my seat and relaxed once again thinking about what the future had in store for us. I seemed to have been doing this a lot of late – giving myself a reality check when I could, maybe because I didn't want to pin my hopes on the idea of starting a new life somewhere until it actually happened. I guess life had taught me that, so in order to protect myself I would do that. I dozed off for a couple of minutes until I was awoken by the aircraft pushing back. We were finally on our way, on our way to London, on our way to start our new life. As the aircraft took off and we climbed steadily I clutched my seat and closed my eyes and said a little pray. Unlike before I didn't feel scared because I knew Allah was watching over us and I knew he would ensure that we arrived safely. I smiled as I looked at my parents sitting there next to me on our way to our new lives the way it was meant to be. In my heart I was happy because we were going to start our new life away from the war, away from the struggles. I can't say I wasn't sad because I would be lying and that wouldn't be right of me. I was a little sad because this had been my home for a couple of years and here I was leaving it. I was also sad because I was leaving all my cousins and all the friends I had made behind. I felt lump in my throat and the tears built up but I kept telling myself that I was strong and that everyone had to move on. I soon settled placing all my trust in Allah the dozed off and only woke up when break-fast was being served. The break-fast was good for aeroplane food except the usual cold cup of tea that I had but I didn't mind too much. After I finished I sat back and fell into a deep sleep dreaming about what London was going to be like. I was woken up by one of the cabin crew who asked me to put my seat in the upright position as we were beginning our descent into Bahrain. As this was a long flight we had to make a stop here to re-fuel and to off-load some passengers. Bahrain is a small Arab country that I didn't know much about so I was a little intrigued about it. We landed and soon the doors opened and you could feel the heat coming from the hot tarmac. Some passengers disembarked and some cleaners came into the aircraft to clean the cabin. New supplies of food and drinks were brought on board and some of the crew were replaced with fresh crew. I watched everyone getting on with their different jobs and occasionally I glanced outside at the aircraft. There were a few aircraft parked there, mainly small ones, there wasn't much happening at the airport. Finally the aircraft pushed back and the engines started up. The aircraft was half empty and there are many window seats available. I immediately made up my mind to grab one as soon as we reach cruising altitude. We roared down the runway and swiftly climb into the air. When we reach cruising altitude and the seat-belt sign went off I quickly jump out of my seat and move across the isle to an empty window seat. I sat there gazing at the wisps of cloud that look as soft as cotton wool that gradually grew until we were flying over a white blanket of cloud. It looked so tranquil and heavenly which made me think of my future. Who was going to meet us at the airport? I hadn't seen my sister Zainab for so many years and I wonder if I would recognise her. All this excitement made me unable to sleep so I just stared at the world outside and let my thoughts carry me away. Mum and dad talked now and again but mostly rested as they are tired. It had been a long tiresome journey so I let them rest. Occasionally I would get up and walk around to start the blood circulating through my legs. There were different types of people onboard and to my surprise even a few children. After a few hours we were told that we were now descending and we should take our seats and fasten our seatbelts. We began our descent away from the warm sunshine into the thick mass of grey clouds. Soon you could see the cars and buildings everywhere. This was something very different for me as I had never seen so many tall ugly buildings that all looked the same. The roads looked big and there were many cars driving up and down them. I couldn't see much out the window as the visibility was poor. We touched down after a few minutes and as the aeroplane taxied to the terminal building I could see so many other aircraft parked there. This was a new experience for me because I had never imagined an airport so big with so many aircraft, but then this was London I thought.

The crew opened the doors and passengers gradually streamed out.

Once we got into the terminal building we managed to follow the other passengers into the immigration hall. The immigration officer was very nice and asked us questions. We then were taken to a room where there was an interpreter ready to translate all the questions asked by the immigration officer. Once our interview was over we were taken to have a medical examination. The doctor was very nice but that wasn't enough to make my heart stop racing. I had never seen these people in my life before and I was supposed to take my scarf off so they could look down my throat, in my ears and shine a bright light in my eyes? I almost fainted when the doctor showed me an injection and began to bring it toward my tiny arm. The interpreter tried to reassure me and tell me that it wouldn't hurt but I didn't believe him. All I felt was a tiny prick and when I looked at my arm I saw the syringe fill up with my blood. I wanted to cry but I couldn't, not in front of all these strangers. Soon after this was complete I had to wait for mum and dad who were in different rooms. This took four hours and when we finally came out into the arrivals hall it was about eight o'clock. We were met by Zainab who was waiting there with her daughter who was only one year old. When mum managed to pick Zainab out from the crowd she burst into tears of joy. Zainab was so happy to see us and she had tears streaming down her cheeks. I had never seen so many different types of people in one place like I did there. Zainab hugged us all and told me that I had grown so much. I felt like I was dreaming, we had finally arrived at our destination, London. Mum and dad were so happy to see Zainab and her daughter Maya. As we made our way to the car park mum and dad talked about the journey here and about how everyone at home was. Once we got to Zainab's house we had something to eat and some hot tea then I went to sleep as I was so tired.

As soon as I put my head down on the pillow I was whisked off to dream land. I slept like a log, not stirring at all that night. Early the next morning I was awoken to get ready for prayers. We prayed as a family which was exactly the way it was always done. Still feeling tired I forced myself to drink a cup of green tea then we all got ready to go for an interview with Ealing Council at nine o'clock. My cousin came to pick us up as he would translate everything for us. This interview had been booked for us so that housing could be arranged for us. We had to wait at the office all day but I didn't mind too much because we had grown acquainted to waiting when we where in Pakistan. At four-thirty in the afternoon they told us that we would have to come back the following day at mid-day when they would have keys for a guesthouse. By this time I was so tired I felt like a walking zombie. When we got home we had dinner and I took a shower and went to bed. I tried to strain my ears to hear what dad was discussing with my cousin but gradually the voices faded away as I fell into a deep sleep. My little body was so tired and needed to rest and adjust to the time difference. I was so happy that we had made it, but I was so tired that all I want to do was sleep. I wanted us to have a place that we can call our home, because Zainab had her own family to look after. The next morning we rose to say our prayers and then got ready to go to the council offices for our mid-day appointment. My cousin came to pick us up and again we set off for the office. When we got there we were told to wait for a couple of minutes and so we did. After waiting about thirty minutes a lady came to apologies to us because they had not been able to get us a guest house and that we would need to come back the next morning at nine. We thanked her as she seemed sincere and left. When we returned to Zainab's house we found that she had guests so we had dinner, said our prayers and then I went upstairs to sleep whilst mum and dad chatted with everyone else. We started the next day with our daily routine and then left for the office because we knew it was important to get there on time as we were using public transport. This was a new experience for me as the buses were so clean and so big and I couldn't control my excitement when we jumped onto a double-decker bus. I had often heard about these but thought that they were just a figment of someone's imagination. There were hardly any people in the bus and this shocked me because in Pakistan the buses were so full that people were almost hanging out of doors. I sat there thinking of my days in Pakistan when I went to town with my aunt who used to fight with the conductors in the buses because they would want her to pay twice. She was a strong woman with a strong character and never let anyone try pull wool over her eyes. We arrived at the office and had to wait for about half an hour to have another interview. After the interview we had to wait for forty-five minutes until the lady came out to tell us that we had to go to an office that was close by to pick up our keys. When I heard this I was happy because we would finally have time to rest. When we got to the office I looked around and it looked exactly like the other one. The lady gave us a piece of paper that had something written on it and then made a few phone calls. When she was through she told us that the guest house was not ready and that the manager said we should go there tomorrow any time after 12 and everything should be ready. I was upset because by now my body needed time to recover because I felt like I had just walked around the whole world and my feet didn't feel like my own. When we got back to Zainab's house she had made dinner and although I was hungry I didn't eat very much because I was tired and also probably because her cooking didn't measure up to mum's cooking which was the best cooking ever. Maya wasn't very well so I had to hold her whilst Zainab was eating because she kept crying. Although I was tired and my head throbbed I tried to put on a happy face because I didn't want her to think that I was annoyed by everything. When she was finished I handed Maya over and began to do the washing up and tidying up of the kitchen because I knew I had to be polite and grateful. This is the way our relationship had always been, she was my oldest sister and I respected her a lot but we had never been close the way sister normally are. I always kept my distance and made sure I didn't get too close to her because I always felt that she didn't really want to know about my problems. When I finished the dishes I took a shower and went to bed but I couldn't get to sleep because Maya was crying the whole night. I kept consoling myself that soon it would be morning and we would be able to get the keys to our guest house and move out of here.

Finally morning came and we all got up to do our daily routine of saying our prayers and then we had our tea. We waited till it was time to go to the guest house. When we arrived there we were met by the manager who showed us our rooms. It was different to what I thought it would be like, because it was a huge flat and my room was on the second floor and my parent's room was on the third. Half of me was worried about this because I had never been really separated from them, because at any time there was at least one of them with me. On the other hand the other half was happy because at least I would have my own space and I could relax. I was looking forward to having a nice long lie in the next morning because I needed it and up till now I couldn't do so because I always had to get up early to get ready. We were given a quick tour of the facilities and I was told that I would have to share the bath-room with many other people. The kitchen was so far and there was no where to sit and have your meal. Instead you would have to come all the way back to you room to eat and then take your plates back there. That night I was scared because I was all alone but once I locked my door and jumped into the nice warm bed I forgot about everything and fell asleep. I had waited for so long for this and finally I was beginning to relax. The next morning was a sunny but cold day and I couldn't get out of bed so I slept until noon something I had never done before.

I used the next couple of days to rest and to observe life around me in this new strange land. I knew at once that life here was going to be very different and to a certain extent difficult as firstly I had yet to learn how to speak English. London was not as great as everyone else made it out to be. I found it to be boring, repetitive and life just moved too fast. I didn't mind too much as I kept telling myself that this was my new home and that I would be fine. The only thing I was not sure about was the weather as it was so unpredictable. As we were unfamiliar to everything the manager introduced us to an Iranian family who became our good friends. They would often cook extra food and bring some over for us and showed us where to go shopping; basically they showed us the everyday things we needed to know in order to survive. Mum and dad were happy to have some company to chat to and get advice from. After about three weeks I was told that I would be going to school. I was happy because finally I would have a chance to go to school like a normal child but part of me was sad and scared as I remembered what had happened back at home when I was at school. I had to go live with Zainab because my school was close to her house and the night before my first day I was so anxious I couldn't sleep. I kept tossing and turning wondering what my first day would be like and praying I would learn English fast and make friends.

The next morning I got ready but couldn't eat much because I had butterflies dancing in my stomach. When Zainab called for me to hurry up as we were about to leave I felt like I was going to be sick but I held my insides in and went down-stairs. That morning Zainab's husband Yacob took me to school even though the school was so close to their house and this made me feel a little relaxed. Once we got there Yacob spoke to the short, fat teacher who looked very friendly and then introduced me and told me that this was Mrs Connor who would be looking after me. As Yacob left I felt like crying and holding on to his leg so he wouldn't leave but I knew I couldn't so I just watched him walk away. Mrs Connor took my hand and led me to a room which was filled with other children who were about my age

– fifteen. She muttered something to me in English and gestured that I should take a seat at the empty table next to me. I wanted to turn around and see what the other children looked like but I couldn't, instead I looked straight ahead. I knew a few English words, but just the basics like Thank-you, please, good-bye etc. The other children sat and talked to each other and I felt so lonely even though I was surrounded by so many people. I sat and watched Mrs Connor's every move wondering when I would be able to go home. My thoughts then wondered off and I thought about mum and dad, what where they doing? A girl came up to me and said something to me, as she seemed friendly all I did was smile because I didn't know what she was saying. The students began to settle down as Mrs Connor began to speak and then I realised she was talking about me because she kept looking at me smiling so I smiled back even though I had no clue what she was talking about. I sat there watching the minutes tick by wondering when it would be time to go home. I felt a little silly sitting in a room where everyone else understood what was going on but me. After a couple of minutes a bell rang and everyone got up and went out the door. I didn't know what was going on or what to do, where to go. I looked around and wanted to ask someone but how when I couldn't? Then the girl who had come up to me before called me to go with her so I did. I was a little relieved that at least she was trying to help me. We went into another class room and sat down. The teacher was a tall gentleman called Mr James and he talked and wrote down something on the board which to me looked like a scribbles drawn by a child. I sat and watched and then he came up to me asked a question. My heart beat fast as I had never had to interact with a European man apart from those at the embassy. He stood there probably expecting me to give him an answer but I just looked at him with a confused look on my face. My new friend who was sitting next to me came to my rescue and then he called my name and I replied with a simple soft 'Yes!' That was my first English word I had used in school. I later came to learn that my new friend's name was Emily. She was blonde with blue eyes and slightly taller than I was. During lunch-time I didn't eat much because my appetite had disappeared. After lunch we had P.E. which was very new to me, but I found it better than the other subjects because all I had to do was copy what everyone else was doing. When P.E. was over I was so tired I felt like just going home and sleeping. We had to go back to Mrs Connor's classroom for the last half and hour. She came up to me and said something and then handed me some books which I put into my bag. The last few minutes seemed to drag on and on and when the bell went off I was relieved that this nightmare had finally come to an end. I could now go home and lick my wounds because I felt today was the worst day of my life. Why had I just been thrown into this environment like this? All day I had felt like I was the prey and a big lion was waiting to pounce on me. Although I felt as low as the leaves that were on the side of the road I tried to be positive and kept telling myself that I would be fine, after all through out the day Emily had taught me a couple of words and I had to start from somewhere. When I was back in Pakistan I had always thought that this would be the best and that everything would be perfect but I guess I was wrong. However I kept my spirits up by telling myself that, 'I have been through so much prior to this and if the war hadn't killed me then this certainly wouldn't , it would only make me stonger'. I knew I had to get through this no matter what.

When I got home everyone wanted to know how my first day was and even though it had felt like the worst day of my life I just smiled and told Zainab and Yacob that I enjoyed it. I went to the bathroom to try to straighten myself up as I felt I was going to start crying and didn't want anyone to see me like this. As a child I had been taught that crying is a sign of weakness and so this was why I could never cry in front of anyone. I pulled myself together then went to help Zainab with the cooking. I knew that I had to put on a happy face and help around the house because it was my duty, my culture and I didn't want to get on Zainab's bad side. So I did the mountain of dishes that had been left in the sink and then cleaned the kitchen. I wanted to go and work on my English because I knew that the only way I would improve was by practising. I missed mum and dad because I was in this strange land and felt so alone. I needed them to encourage me and tell me that everything would be alright. What were they doing? Were they missing me as much as I missed them?

The next morning was different as Yacob didn't take me to school; instead Zainab stood by her front door and told me to run as fast as I could to school whilst she watched me. I hated running because running always made me remember life during the war. I didn't want to run anymore, I just wanted to walk and enjoy every step of my life. At school I found myself sitting all alone because Emily had abandoned me because her best-friend had come to school that day so I was of no use to her anymore. I sat at my desk and just kept to myself not wanting to make eye contact with anyone. Lessons began and again I sat and watched only understanding a few simple words. When the class finished and we had to change classrooms all I did was follow Emily who was in the same class as I was for all my subjects. She must have been really been bad at English, maths and the other subjects as we were in the same class. She was beautiful but not very intelligent and I didn't want to be like her at all. The first couple of days at school became routine as I would go to school and spent the day just day dreaming or looking around. When I got home I was so tired and just wanted to relax and watch TV but I knew that I had to do my chores. There was a pile of ironing to do and so I got to work. By the time Zainab started cooking dinner I was almost finished but it had taken me almost the whole afternoon. After dinner I washed the dishes and cleaned the kitchen.

The following week Mrs Connor smiled at me and called out another name that sounded like a Muslim name to a girl who was sitting on the opposite end of the classroom. She replied with a polite 'yes!' Mrs Connor spoke to her and she stood up and walked over to me and sat next to me. I tried to look at her with the corner of my eye as I didn't want her to know that I was looking at her. She touched my arm to get my attention and said 'Salaam! Esmam Nour. Esmetun chi ye?' I couldn't believe my ears. I suddenly felt a warm happy feeling in my chest and I smiled and said, 'Salaam! Esmam Nayia.' She had long jet black hair, and had such beautiful green eyes, and like me she wasn't very tall. I was excited that at least now I could have someone to talk to and hopefully she could help me with my school work. She was very friendly and helped me a lot. During lunch time I sat with her and we talked about which region she was from and how she came here. She promised to help me and this made me feel better. However there were some classes that she was in a different class so I was stuck with Emily and her friends. I didn't mind because there weren't that many classes that we had separately anyway. Over the next couple of weeks Nour helped me with my English and Maths and at times I felt like giving up but I knew I couldn't.

After a week Zainab and Yacob asked me if I had meet a girl called Nour as she was supposed to be in my class. I wondered how they knew this and then they told me they knew the family. Why didn't Zainab tell me this? Anyway I just replied with a simply 'yes'. My instincts had told me not to go into a deep conversation with Zainab about my new found friend because she would ask me too many questions. I continued going to school for the next two weeks then we broke up for summer holidays.

Although I had only been in school for a short time I was glad the holidays had come so I could relax and practise my English and most important of all, I could go home to mum and dad who I had missed so much. The weather was beautiful and I enjoyed the sunshine which reminded me of the heat in my native land. When I returned to the guest house not much had changed but that comforted me. Although initially I didn't like this place now I felt like I would rather be here than at Zainab's house. It felt good to lie on my bed and enjoy the peace and quiet that I had got little of before. I was looking forward to dinner as I had missed mum's cooking and dad. They were so happy that I was back and dad couldn't stop asking me questions about how school was. He told me how proud he was of me as he knew it was difficult to start again. It felt good to hear dad say that and I made a promise to myself then, 'that I would always strive to achieve more.' During dinner dad announced the news that my older sister Yasmeen and her son Babak were coming over for summer holidays to visit us from America. I was very happy as I couldn't remember what my sister and nephew looked like. I couldn't wait and hoped the good weather would continue. My first night in a long time in my bed was like heaven as I quickly forgot about how hard I had found school and just enjoyed the feeling of freedom. After a few minutes I was fast asleep dreaming about the arrival of my sister, would she remember what I looked like? I woke up late the next morning and felt great. I wanted to make the most of my holiday and knew that I would have to try learning some more English before I went back to school. The Iranian family the Mahmoodys' who had become our friends welcomed me back as I walked to the kitchen. Mrs Mahmoody who we called Mrs Moody invited me to go shopping with her and I accepted as I didn't have much to do. On the way there she showed me different areas and told me how to say more words in English. When returned I thanked her for inviting me to go out with her and for teaching me more English words and she told me that I should come over the next day so she could show me more. This is how I wanted to spend some of my summer learning how to read the books from school to improve my English. We started with the basics of the alphabet 'A', 'B', 'C' and how to count to ten and gradually I learnt how to write my name. I found this especially hard because I was used to writing from right to left not the opposite way. I didn't have these lessons everyday as Mrs Moody was sometimes busy.

Finally the day came for Yasmeen and Babak to arrive and I was so excited that I must have changed about three times because I wanted to look good. We had cleaned and cooked the day before so everything was perfect and now we all sat together waiting for them to arrive. Mum and dad didn't appear as anxious as I was or perhaps because they were better at being patient than I was. When they finally arrived everyone was happy and mum and Yasmeen shed tears of joy because it had been many years since we had seen Yasmeen. She was everything I thought she would be because I couldn't remember much about her. She gave me a big hug and loads of kisses. Babak was now a grown man who towered over me. He was older than me though but he had changed a considerable amount since the last time I saw him. Yasmeen was so happy to see me that she kept hugging and smiling at me. Laughter and love filled the room making it almost electrical and as we sat to eat dinner there was so much to talk about. We eat until we were stuffed and Yasmeen praised mum about her excellent cooking and how she had missed it. Babak also agreed that the meal was excellent as he sipped his drink. Mum had made lamb, chicken kebabs, rice, aubergines, hot naan bread with a fresh green salad with loads of mint and lemon juice. After dinner I washed up and then made some green tea for everyone to have with desert. Yasmeen told us about America and how different it was. We talked till about ten when mum and dad said good-night as they were tired and need to go to bed. Yasmeen and Babak would stay in my room with me and I liked this idea as I would have company. We continued to talk and Yasmeen told me about their journey. She told me that she had missed me and that she was looking forward to spending time with me because we didn't have the chance before. She had moved to America a long time ago and hence we never really had had a chance to bond. Babak went to sleep and we continued to talk about life. We got ready for bed and at about midnight we went to sleep. I was so tired because I had spent the previous day helping mum and I guess the excitement had made me tired. I fell asleep thinking about what we would do tomorrow.

I got up early to say my prayers and help mum get break-fast ready for everyone. Yasmeen and Babak were fast asleep and I didn't want to wake them by opening the curtains so I left them to sleep as they had to rest from the long journey. As I walked to the kitchen I looked outside and it looked like it would be a bright warm day. Mum was already making breakfast and I helped her even though there was not much to do. As there was not really anywhere to sit and have a meal we had resorted to eating in my room. Mum asked me to check if everyone was up so I set off down the long corridor to my room. When I opened the door the morning light from the windows flooded the room and there Yasmeen and Babak were already awake and ready for breakfast. I got the room ready for breakfast and Yasmeen helped me by bringing the food from the kitchen. Dad came down and joined everyone and we sat and enjoyed the food and each other's company. Dad told us that today we would spend the day at home because Yasmeen and

Babak needed to rest. I wanted us to go out and enjoy the sun but I knew dad was right so I thought I would use this time to practice my English. After breakfast I went to Mrs Moody and spent an hour with her doing some work as I couldn't concentrate because I wanted Yasmeen to wake up so we could talk. Later on when they had woken up we had a chance to chat again and she asked me how I was getting on at school. I told her that I was finding it hard because it was so different and she said that she would help me. Over the next couple of days they rested and when Yasmeen had a chance we talked. Mum took Yasmeen to go see Zainab but I decided to stay with dad and Babak. Babak could speak English fluently and he began to help me learn. I enjoyed his company as he told me many stories about America and his friends. As the days went by and school holidays were drawing to an end I didn't want to go back to school because I was scared of going back to that environment of not understanding. I knew that I didn't want to go back to Zainab's house because I felt that I would be better off here so when dad asked me when I wanted to go I told him I didn't. He didn't seem to mind and then after thinking for a while he said that if I really wanted to stay then here I could, but I had to make sure I learn how to get to school on my own.

Quickly I grabbed Babak by the hand and led him to the door to execute my plan. I had to show dad that I was responsible and able to find my way. Babak had never lived in London but as he could speak perfect English I knew he could get me anywhere. As we were going down the stairs we meet Mrs Moody who advised us what buses we had to take. Armed with that information we set off on our mission. We navigated our way through the busy streets until we found the bus stop with the correct bus we were to take was supposed to stop. I knew I would be fine with Babak because he could always find out how to get home by asking and like a big brother I knew he would protect me from the 'world'. We quickly made our way on to the bus and sat in my favourite position, the top deck. As we went past many different buildings Babak told me what they were in Pashto and then would tell me in English. It was a bright day and this made everything look so radiant, such a change from winter which I hadn't yet experienced but had heard about. Since the day we arrived here in London I could have counted the number of clear skies, bright days like this one. This was one thing I missed about Pakistan because this weather was so unpredictable here and miserable that it made me feel the same. We then changed buses and after about twenty minutes we alighted on to the pavement and walked towards a building that looked familiar to me. I then realised that we were there right in front of the school that I dreaded returning to. Babak looked proud that we had found our way without getting lost and that it didn't take us as long as we had initially thought. He was grinning from ear to ear and although I didn't like the building I too felt proud because I had made it here by bus even though I was being accompanied it felt good. We turned around and made our way back to the bus stop to return home. I made a note of significant landmarks that I would remember so I wouldn't get lost when I began this journey on my own. When we got home dad was delighted at our success and he asked Babak to accompany me to school for the first few days which made me feel better because with him by my side I knew I was safe.

The last couple of days of my holiday went by so fast and I wished I could take the batteries out of the clock so the time would stop but reality hit me – I had to accept that it would be difficult at first but I would one day enjoy school. It would soon be time for Yasmeen and Babak to leave even though it felt like it had only been a week since their arrival. The first day of school came and Babak and I left early to give sufficient time for traffic jams which were a normal thing in that area. We got onto the bus and I could feel my stomach turning inside out. I kept trying to make small talk with Babak so I would stop thinking about going back to school. There was a lot of traffic but I knew we would be fine because we had allocated enough time just in case we got stuck in traffic. We got to school in time and I felt like telling Babak that I was not feeling well so I could go home again but then I thought that dad would be disappointed with me if I did so I stayed. Babak told me he would pick me up after school and left. So there I was in this ugly block shaped building I had been dreaded all summer. As I was going through the front doors I saw Nour walking down the corridor so I followed her as I couldn't shout her name out in the corridor and draw attention to myself. I just wanted to be invisible, but I guess that would have been difficult because I was so different to everyone else and also because I wore a full hijab and my English wasn't that good. I knew that I had to wear my hijab as this was normal for me but for everyone else it wasn't normal and I guess that made me feel uncomfortable as other pupils would constantly stare like I had three heads or something. I felt like asking them,' didn't your mothers ever teach you not to stare?' However as much as I would have like to express my anger by saying something like that

I knew that sooner or later they would get used to the idea and I would stop feeling uncomfortable. As I went into the classroom Nour saw me and gestured to me to come and sit next to her so I did. I was glad that at least she was here and I had someone who could understand me and therefore help me. We had a new teacher called Mr. Brown and Nour said he was very nice and was always ready to help anyone who needed help. I hoped that this was the man who would help me improve my English. He was very well spoken and had bushy eyebrows that reminded me of a cousin back in Pakistan. The day begun with maths class and I was in a different class to Nour so I sat there all alone bored out of my mind. Apart from that I was upset because I felt excluded. In English class I always felt depressed and even though I had learnt a lot during the holidays I was not confident and never wanted to try because I was scared that I would be wrong and everyone would laugh at me so I remained quiet. As much as I hated school though, I never missed a day even when I was sick because somewhere inside I knew that this was the only way I would learn.

Apparently according to Nour, Mrs Connor had left our school and was now working elsewhere. When I heard this I was upset because who was going to help me now? I felt like I had a special bond with her and now she had left, was I expected to start all over again? I must be honest the thought of throwing in the towel did cross my mind because it seemed like the odds were against me no matter what. Nour told me not to worry because there was always Mr Brown who was very good at helping out students. During lunch we went to see him and I stood next to Nour as she explained that I needed help. Mr Brown accepted and smiled at me and told me to come to the classroom everyday between lunchtime for half an hour. This made me very optimistic and happy. I was finally going to start improving my English, I was at peace. So the very next day I looked forward to the class at lunch time and as soon as the bell went for lunch I rushed to Mr Brown's classroom and knocked on the door. There were two other girls sitting there when I entered. Mr Brown asked me to sit down and then he handed me a book with the alphabet and numbers. I knew the alphabet and how to count as I had practised all this during my holiday. He read out the alphabet and gestured to me to say it out loud. My heart was beating faster because I didn't feel confident enough to recite the alphabet to him in front of the other two girls but after taking a deep breathe I began. Mr Brown was very surprised and encouraged me to continue. He had a big smile on his face which made me feel at ease. After I was finished he asked the other two to do the same but they didn't do as well as I had done. I was proud of myself; I had climbed a step closer to the top of the mountain and even though I was still very far from the peak I was going to get there. The time went by so fast and soon it was time to leave as I had to have my lunch before the afternoon programs started. I went to the canteen and had some chips and beans because I knew that they were halal. I didn't like beans from the first time I had them, they just tasted so horrible but I guess it was either chips and beans or just plain chips. For the rest of the week Babak accompanied me to and from school. I was anxious about the following week as I knew that Yasmeen and Babak were leaving over the week-end so I would have to make this journey on my own and that thought made me uneasy. When the day came for them to leave we were all very upset. We had enjoyed having them here and I had felt like I had an older brother to help me with adjusting to life in London and I had enjoyed spending time with my sister. Mum and Dad were equally distraught because having them here had brightened up their days. Yasmeen and Babak like everyone else cried because they had enjoyed their visit and also because they didn't know when the next time we would meet would be. As their taxi slowly drove off I felt like running after it and telling them that they didn't have to go and that we wanted them to stay. It was the three of us again.

On Sunday evening I prepared all my school books and my uniform. I was no longer anxious but excited because I was going to make this journey on my own. The next morning I got up early, got ready and mum and dad told me to be careful then I left. As I sat on the bus I realised that I recognised a number of similar landmarks that I had mark on my first trip with Babak. When I got closer to school I pressed the bell and the bus came to a gentle stop and I jumped out. The feeling I had when I stepped on to the pavement was like a ball of fire burning in my chest. I had found my way to school and not got lost and this made me proud. I wanted to shout it out in the streets so everyone would know. I guess this little accomplishment gave me a little more confidence. Slowly I gained confidence to try speak the little bit of English I had learnt because Mr Brown probably gave me confidence and told me that in order to improve I would have to take the risk of making mistakes. Sometimes I was embarrassed to go up and ask for help with something if Nour was sitting next to me because I didn't want her to think that I didn't appreciate or value her help. When I got home mum and dad were happy that I had returned safely. Dad was very proud of me and said that I would get far in life because I was always the most determined child. This became my daily routine and soon I knew my way home very well. One afternoon I returned to find my parents rather feeling homesick because they spent much of their time in doors as the weather was getting rather chilly. They asked me if I wanted to go back to Pakistan and even though I felt like saying yes I told them I couldn't go back. So with my answer they knew they had to stay and look after me even though the hated this country as they didn't have many friends and because it had begun to get cold. Soon Ramadan came and I found it easy to fast through out the day as unlike in Pakistan the days here were shorter and because it was cold you didn't need to drink any water. It was difficult in the morning though when I would get up early to go to the kitchen for Suhur as sometimes the kitchen door was locked because the manager's wife would not have woken up early enough to open it. I was not alone because many people had to do the same. So my body got used to being able to not have anything in the morning and I would last the whole day until I got home to break my fast. It was good to come home after a long day at school to the place I had to come to know as home and join my family in prayer and go through the ritual of Iftar. This time in any Muslim's life makes them grateful for everything they have. It made me proud to have come all the way to London and still keep the values I was raised with. When Eid came it was very different to what I had known all my life but we still celebrated and enjoyed each other's company. We had been fasting on the day of Eid not knowing that instead we should be celebrating when we heard the announcement on the radio. We then had to break our fast and let the celebrations begin even though we had not really had any time to prepare because we didn't know what day it would fall on. My first Eid, in a foreign land, away from my friends and extended family but I didn't mind because I was with my parents. In the afternoon Zainab and Yacob came over to wish us Eid Mubarak and as we sat and enjoyed the delicious feast that mum had thrown together at the last minute whilst we reminisced about old times.

A couple of weeks after Eid celebrations we received some good news, the council had found us a house to live in. It all sounded really good because we would finally have a place to call our own. I was excited and happy that we would finally start to rebuild our lives in our new home. No more sharing a kitchen, no more sharing a bathroom with many other people, no more having to walk all the way up stairs to go see mum and dad. I would finally have my own room and we would have a garden and not have to share it with so many other people. So one afternoon Yacob picked dad up and took over to the council office to sought out the paperwork. Unfortunately dad didn't get a chance to view the house and just had to sign the papers and was told he would receive the keys the day before we move in. So when he returned he gave us the good news and told us we were moving in five days time. Mum had mixed feeling about everything because dad had not had the chance to view the house and area before hand and didn't know where it was. How were we going to find our way around? How was I going to get to school? Who would show me the way? Suddenly I began to see mum's concern and

I was excited but a little apprehensive about moving away from familiar territory. The day came for us to move and Mrs Moody helped us pack everything and together with her husband took us to our new house. As we drove into the area cold shivers ran down my spine as it was not what I expected. There were papers blowing in the wind everywhere and the buildings were dirty, old, depressing. When we arrived at the house and I looked at it and my heart sank, oh my God was this it? We had waited so long only to be brought to this. I was angry with dad for not coming to view the house before, even though I knew it wasn't his fault. Looking at this place I would have preferred to have stayed in the guest house even though I had to continue sharing the kitchen and bathroom. I looked at dad and could tell by the look on his face that he was not happy with what he saw. Mum was not pleased either and kept asking if there was anyway we could change our minds and go back to the guest house. When dad opened the door it was hard to believe that this house was in an area like this. The house was brand new and still had plastic around many of the structures like the bathroom. The house was a lot better on the inside than the outside, I guess because the area was bad. Mr Moody had to make a few trips by car from the guest house to our house bringing all our belongings for us. There was nothing in the house and it was clear that we would have to start the hectic process of buying furniture. The house didn't even have a carpet on the floor and I wondered how we would survive during winter on this cold floor. We had no beds; no chairs to sit on, the rooms were just bare. I was worried because until we would be able to start buying furniture we would have nothing. This brought back memories of the night my house was burnt down.

I felt vulnerable and naked not knowing what we were going to do to get by. We brought our bags inside and began unpacking the little belongings we had. Mrs moody could see that this house had come with nothing and so she went home and cooked us a few dishes to eat as we didn't even have a stove. This was such a nice thing for her to do. These were good people with good hearts; good friends and we appreciated them. We began unpacking and we were soon finished. We sat on the floor and mum and dad discussed what they would do the next day. That night was a difficult night as I was not used to sleeping on the floor. I could feel the cold coming through the thick layer of cushions and blankets I had put beneath me. I guess I felt cold because there wasn't any furniture in the room which left me feeling exposed and also because there was no carpet to break the cold frosty air that blew in from the crack under the door.

I eventually drifted off to sleep and was woken up in the morning by a strange sound. It sounded like the something coming through the slit in the door for the letters. I knew it wasn't letters because we had not informed anyone about our move. I woke up and peered round my bedroom door to have a look at what had made this weird noise. There on the bare floor was a pile of sand mixed with bits of dirt and stones. Where had this come from, I wondered? Maybe it had blown in with the draft from outside because our garden was very bare and exposed. I got a broom and dustpan and immediately started to clean up the dirt still thinking about what had happened. When my parents awoke dad decided to go out and have a look at the area and find out vital information like where the closest shops where and so on. Mum and I remained behind and gave the house a through cleaning and then arranged everything in an orderly fashion. When dad returned he told us that we had to go out to the shops so we could buy a couple of items like more blankets and some food that was easy to prepare and keep. We did a couple of trips up and down as the shops were not to far each time bringing back the necessities. Later on that afternoon Mrs Moody returned to see how we were getting along. She brought us delicious, hot dinner which we laid out to share as well as two chairs and a small table. I had forgotten all about school until she reminded me that I must go to bed early on Sunday evening as the journey to school would be longer. I was lucky our neighbours the Khans' from across the street had come to welcome us to the area. They were from Pakistan and had lived in this area for a while now. Mrs Khan asked me where I went to school and when I told her, her face lit up. She told me her niece went to the same school and that I should come over in the morning so that we could go together so I could learn to find my way. I wished Babak was with me like last time to help me and show me the way. I listened carefully as she explained and made sure I made her write everything down in Farsi and English just in case I got lost. That night I slept like a baby not stirring the whole night because I was warm and exhausted from the day's hard work. I don't remember what I dreamt because I was too tired. The next morning I woke up feeling fresh and ready to take everything that the day was going to throw at me. We had break-fast and went out to the high street to purchase a few items for our house. We managed to purchase a nice stove that came complete with an oven and some cooking utensils. The stove was going to be delivered to us in a couple of days so with that taken care of we shopped for things that we would need like crockery and cutlery. We made a couple of trips taking things home and going back for more. We returned from the last trip each carrying heavy shopping bags filled with everything we would need to start building our new house into a home. When we got home and opened the front door we noticed a pile of dirt like the one before. I felt a little frustrated now as I didn't know where this dirt was coming from and we all stood there and pondered over this mystery. I began to clean it up and then helped mum put everything away. We had dinner and dad sat listening to the radio, whilst I did the washing up and mum moved things around. There was a knock at the door and dad stood up to see who it was. There on our doorstep stood Yacob and our suitcases we had left at Zainab's house. He came in and we helped him bring them all in as well. I was happy because at last I was re-united with some of my belongings. At last I could change clothes as much as I wanted to as I had been restricted until now.

The next morning I got up early to get ready for school as I wanted to get there on time. I went and waited for Mrs Khan's friend's daughter Amna, who was going to show me the way. When I got there Amna's mother told me to sit down and wait as Amna was not ready yet. I didn't want to be late as this was not my custom, but what was I to do? I sat staring at the minutes tick by on the big clock that hung on the wall in the kitchen, wondering when this girl would hurry up. I hoped she knew a fast way to get to school because we didn't have much time. Finally she emerged from the bedroom and introduced herself, apologising frantically about her bad time keeping. We left and went to wait at the bus stop for the bus which came almost immediately. We made general chit-chat on the bus mainly about how she had adjusted to life here. One thing that annoyed me about her was the way she kept asking me the same question over and over again, 'Why do you wear a scarf?' I felt like shouting, 'Come on you know why I wear a scarf, the question you should be asking yourself is, why don't I wear a scarf?' I expected her as a Muslim to know why we wore scarves and to respect my decision to wear one. Was she trying to influence me not to be myself, to forget my culture? I felt like she had done this and wanted me to join her but I couldn't. Finally we got to Ealing Broadway train station where we caught a train to Acton. The journey had been a lot longer than what I was used to but we finally got there in the end even though we were late. Amna didn't care about our punctuality she just thought it was 'cool', but I didn't. I wanted to be early because I needed time to find my classroom because it was never in the same place. School began and things were the same as they were everyday except when lunch-time came because this was my time to learn and improve. I always looked forward to lunch! When school was finished I waited for Amna to come out then we went home and I carefully looked at buildings I could use as landmarks because I wasn't going to be late everyday, I knew I had to find my own way to school. On my returned home I found mum and dad waiting for me so we could have dinner together. After I had dinner I did the washing up and then went and sat down on the rug we had bought and there I did my homework. It took me a while to complete it and I wasn't even sure if I had done it right or not but at least I had completed it and by doing this I would learn from my mistakes. I was actually quiet proud of myself because I had attempted every question and didn't mind if I wasn't going to get everything right. When I was finished I felt like there was nothing to do because we had no television. We only had a radio but when you have become used to watching television it's hard to re-adjust to not seeing what it is you are listening to so I didn't bother even trying. I tried to read my English books but I found that my concentration was easily broken probably because I was tired. I decided to just take a bath and go straight to sleep because I knew it would be an early. I just hopped that Amna would be on time so we could leave enough time for our journey. I fell asleep relatively quickly, I guess I hadn't realised how tired I was.

The next morning I awoke early and got ready and said my prayers to Allah that I would have a good day. I put my oversized uniform on the same way I had done everyday and had a cup of green tea. Once I was done I left home and headed for the bus stop where Amna and I had agreed to meet. I sat on the bench and waited as I was five minutes early, watching the different cars drive by. These streets were nothing like the streets of Kandahar or even Quetta. Although the roads here were probably better the atmosphere was totally different, at this time of the morning in Kandahar most people would be up getting on with their daily lives. The morning air would be lightly scented with the smell of freshly baked bread and the warm sunshine would fall on the dew covered grass. Here I was breathing the cold, frosty air of London which made me feel even colder than I was. My toes were so cold that at one stage I glanced down to make sure I was wearing my shoes and socks. Where was Amna? I just put my hands in my pockets to keep warm and prayed she would hurry up or we would be late for school yet again and I would probably be frozen but the time she decided to grace me with her presence. I tried not to get angry but I was couldn't help myself, why was she always late even when we had arranged to meet at a certain time? Was she playing me for a fool? Was I a fool for standing here so early freezing my toes off? 'No!' I kept telling myself, I wasn't a fool I was someone who believed in keeping promises. It wasn't right that she had made a promise and then left me here waiting for such a long time. I checked my watch and by now I had been waiting for at least thirty minutes. I turned round and saw Amna walking toward me. At that moment I just wanted to go and shout at her but that's not what my parents taught me so I just kept my anger within and smiled. She apologised and made up some lousy excuse about her mother or something. We caught the next bus and by the time we got to the train station there was so much traffic. We just about made it to school on time but in my standards I was late because I still had to find my classroom and for me this was always a task. The day went by rather fast and during lunch time for thirty minutes I went to my class to get extra help. Nour always waited for me in the canteen so at least when I was finished I went to sit with her. Finally the school day came to an end and then again I had to wait for Amna who never left on time because she was so busy talking to her friends. The way home looked very similar now and I could pick out my landmarks. I'm sure I could go to school alone now or could I?

I couldn't wait to get home and throw my uniform off as I wanted to jump into something warm and wrap myself in a blanket as I was cold. I was surprised when I saw almost all the eastern people walking around with no jumpers on and here I was freezing. It was mid autumn now and the roads were littered with orange red leaves and the trees were almost bear. They actually looked rather weird unlike the leaves scattered everywhere which I thought were beautiful. Everyone kept telling me that this was not even close to winter! When I got home I changed and got ready for dinner which we always tried to eat together. Mum and dad had been shopping and bought a few rugs which we spread in the lounge and in our bedrooms so that we could sleep on them and not be exposed to the cold floor. They told me they had also picked out a carpet and two beds one of which was going to be mine. This cheered me up as we were making progress and I thought we were adapting well considering we had just moved in. I washed the dishes and cleaned the kitchen and then started on my homework. Once I was done I decided to just go have a bath then straight to bed and rest, but mainly because I was bored, it was only half past seven. I guess the day had taken a toil on my small body which made me go out like a light. Within minutes I was fast asleep.

The next morning I got up slightly earlier than usual and made sure I got ready quickly. I said my prayers and had my cup of tea and left at about seven fifteen. I was determined to get to school on my own and I wanted to give myself enough time. As I got to the bus stop the bus came and I jumped on making sure I sat near the window on the top deck so I could see my landmarks. I changed bus and proceeded towards Ealing Broadway station where I got off and caught the train. When the train stopped at Acton town I knew I was almost there. When I got to my station I wanted to jump for joy. I had made it to the station, and I knew it wasn't far to reach my school now. I came out of the station and walked to school slowly as I still had forty-five minutes. I arrived at school within fifteen minutes which still left me with plenty time to find my class. I walked in a couple of classrooms checking in each to see if my fellow classmates where there and walked out when I didn't recognise anyone. I finally found my class and sat down and relaxed, I had made it on my own. A great sense of relief and joy came over me, I had done on my own and it felt great! I couldn't wait to get home and tell mum and dad that I could now find my own way to school. Today seemed brighter probably because I was in a good mood and felt invincible! School went on as usual and when home time came I quickly said bye to Nour and left. I walked to the train station quickly and waited about 5minutes for the train. I sat down and looked out the window as the train went passed all my landmarks. We pulled into my station and I got up and went out to find my bus. I could see my bus pulling away from the bus stop and I felt like running after it but then I saw another one heading towards the bus stop. Looking at the traffic I knew I would make it to the stop in time and so I walked at normal pace and as I got there the bus stopped and I got on. Within minutes I was at home, which was good for me because at least now I could relax and help mum prepare dinner. I guess my afternoons and evenings were always the same as I didn't have any friends nearby that I could spend time with and we had not yet been able to buy a TV so I just had to be content with what I had, my books, my parents and my bed. When I walked into the kitchen I was surprised to see the new stove that we had been waiting. At last we could have a nice hot meal whenever we wanted to. Up until now we had relied on using Mrs Khan's stove and fridge. Mum and dad told me that soon the beds would arrive and the fridge was on its way. The rest of the week went on as usual and I was happy when the week-end came. On Friday night I looked back at the week and I was filled with pride because I had managed to get myself to school and back.

On Saturday I woke up late and found the house deserted, probably because mum and dad had gone out shopping. As I was cleaning the house I noticed a pile of sand and dirt by the front door. This was the same as the pile I had found before, but I still hadn't figured out where it had come from. I cleaned it up and my parents returned with bags of shopping. I wasn't sure where they intended putting all this stuff as there was things like milk and meat that needed a fridge and I didn't think Mrs Khan would have enough space in her fridge. Dad told me to stop worry as our fridge was being delivered within the hour. We packed everything away and then sat in the lounge and talked. My parents had woken up early to go shopping and had gone passed the shop that we bought the fridge from and they said that they could deliver it that same day. The hour went by and there was no sign of them, and I grew anxious. What were going to do with all this fresh produce if they didn't turn up? I went to my room and sat on my rug and read my English books. After about two hours there was a knock at the door. For a moment I wonder who it could be because I had forgotten about the delivery we were supposed to have. When dad opened the door a man stood there and asked him to sign for the fridge which he did and then two other men who wore black turbines carried it in. they placed it in the kitchen in a corner just next to the stove and plugged it in and then left. I jumped up and helped mum examine it then start cleaning it and finally it was ready for us to begin to put our fresh produce in it. The rest of the week end I spent doing my homework and relaxing. I was glad we had a fridge now because I could now enjoy having ice cold drinks which I often craved. Autumn was now coming to an end and I could tell that winter was on its way, as the sun was setting so early.

Monday morning came and I had to get up to get ready for school. I left home and took the bus to the station and then the train. I always made sure I gave myself enough time because I knew that sometimes there was lots of traffic. I arrived at school with plenty of time to spare. The day at school went by relatively fast which was good and I felt I was beginning to understand a little more English. When the final bell rang to signal the end of school I packed my bag, said 'bye' to my friends and left. When I got home I was happy with myself and convinced that I knew the way. It had begun to get colder now and on some days it felt like the sun had not even come out because it was so dark and gloomy. This made me feel so depressed and like I didn't want to go to school, when I left in the morning it was dark and when I returned it was the same. I often sat on rug and thought of life back in Pakistan and what my cousins I had left behind were doing. Did they miss me? Well the day at school went by fast and as I made my way to the train station I all I could think about was having a hot cup of tea and sitting near the radiator because I was so cold. I waited for a couple of minutes before the train came and I did not hesitate when the doors opened because I knew it was a lot warmer inside there than where I was standing. The train left the station and we begun our journey. This train normally called at each station so I was surprised when it didn't stop at the next station, but then I thought it probably didn't stop because that station was shut. To my surprise it didn't call at any of the stations it usually did and this made me a little uneasy. Would it call at my stop I kept thinking? The train raced on and my palms became sweatier and my heart beat faster. I was confident that it would call at my stop because it always did. There was an old man snoring away at the far carriage and a mother with her baby just a couple of seats away from me. They all looked like they knew that this train would not call at any of the stations until it got to its destination. This train was on a one way track and I was stuck on it. Where was it going to take me? As I looked outside nothing looked familiar and the fact that it got darker early didn't help because I couldn't really see perfectly. I should have reached my station by now. Maybe it was taking a different route? I wanted to ask the lady sitting near me when this train would stop but she was too busy playing with her baby and would she even understand what I was saying? By now I realised that this train was not going to call at my station and I didn't know where it was taking me. I looked at my watch and it was already five o'clock. Mum and dad would be worried as I was usually home by this time. How was I going to find my way home? Where was I? Finally the train pulled into a station and I saw everyone getting out of the train. This was probably the last stop but I was unsure about what to do next. If I got out where would I go to find a train home? If I stayed would this train take me back to where I had come from? I was scared and I could hear my heart beating like crazy. I was lost, all alone in a foreign land, no one to help me! There was a large lump in my throat and I felt the tears building up in my eyes. I got up and exited the train not knowing where I was going. My eyes felt like they were burning because they could no longer hold the reservoir of tears, and then the first tears streamed down my pink cheeks. Who could help me? I walked up the stairs trying to blink away the tears which were making my vision blurred. From the little I could make out I could tell that I had never seen this area before. As I walked away from the stairs I had come up, there stood a Sikh man with a long white beard and blue turbine. I knew I had to use this opportunity to speak to him because he was my only chance of getting home. I was scared to speak to him but then I guess the thought of never being reunited with my parents and being lost forever made me realise that I had to do it. As I began to make my way toward him my mouth became so dry that when I tried to open it to speak no words came out, instead the tears now rolled down my cheeks even faster. He looked at me and smiled and that's when the words came out. I spoke to him in Urdu carefully explaining what had happened. He looked concerned and then told me not to worry that he would help me and he did by giving me directions. He was very nice and told me to dry my eyes, be strong and that everything would be okay. He directed me to a train on the opposite platform from the on I had arrived on and told me to catch the next train, which I did. After drying my eyes I told myself that I would be fine; I would find my way home. Soon the train finally came to Ealing Broadway station and when I looked at the big clock on the wall it was already eight thirty. The tears had disappeared and I just wanted to get home to my parents. As I stood waiting for the bus I could feel the cold biting my toes and fingers. My school jumper was not that warm so there I stood with my teeth rattling. In Pakistan it never got this cold even during winter so this was a first for me. At last the bus came and I got on and sought for refuge against the cold, a seat far away from the door as possible. In order to catch another bus which would take me straight home I had to get off again and wait in the cold until it came. It was so cold that I couldn't feel my fingers and toes by now and my face and nose were so dry. The only way I could keep warm was by squeezing my-self tight but it wasn't working. Finally the bus came and it seemed to take forever to get home as I kept looking at my watch which appeared as if time was just not moving. I felt like I was catching a cold as all the symptoms where there, sneezing, runny nose and a dry throat. My stomach was complaining too as I hadn't eaten since lunch time. As the bus approached my stop I could see a figure that resembled mum. When I got off the bus I saw that it was her and I felt so relieved. I had made it; my nightmare had at last come to an end. Mum hugged me so tight and tears rolled down her cheeks as she told me that they had been worried about me. I felt so weak and tired that I couldn't cry with her. I was just happy I was back with them again. All I wanted to do was go home and eat, have a bath and jump into bed. Mum was so worried about me because it was clear to see that I had been a victim of bad weather. My lips were so dry that they felt frozen that they started bleeding. We walked back home and when we opened the door the warmth of the house hit my frozen little body. Dad rushed towards me and hugged me and told me he was worried sick and was glad that I was safe now. I was glad to be surrounded by familiar things especially my parents, that I found myself now appreciated the smallest of things like the smell of my house. Mum quickly made me a cup of hot tea and warmed up my dinner. It was very warm in the house so I didn't need to sit right near the radiator whilst I ate my dinner and the tea warmed up my cold fingers so I began to regain feeling in them. Mum ran a hot bath for me whilst I ate my dinner which I couldn't wait to jump into. The hot bubble bath made me relax and forget about the bad day I had had. The day's events had tired me out that I even forgot about doing any homework and just headed straight for bed. As soon as I put my head down on the pillow I drifted off into dream land until mum woke me up the next morning to get ready for school.

I got ready for school the same way I did every other day but today I wanted to leave slightly earlier. Mum and dad were reluctant for me to go on my own, insisting that I should wait for Amna so at least I wouldn't get lost, but I turned down that idea. How could I wait for someone who always made me late I told them? Finally they saw things from my point of view and told me to be careful. I left home not to sure if I was doing the right thing, should I wait for Amna and be late for school or should I take my chances and find my own way? I guess my strong character won me over and I decided to go with the second decision- find my own way. This was the way I was, I would rather do things on my own to develop myself. The bus came straight away and I began my journey to school. When I arrived at Ealing Broadway I got off the bus but instead of going to the train station I decided to walk to school as I was not going to take my chances getting lost again. My school was not that far from here and I kind of knew my way there so I decided to take my shot at that rather than the train. It was so cold that I could feel the cold breeze on my nose as it came through my scarf but I had made up my mind and so I began the walk. I only knew one route to get to school walking and although it was long compared to the train I knew I had to do this. Looking at my watch I had about forty-five minutes to get there before school started so I walked briskly so I wouldn't be late and also to keep warm. Many cars went passed and I saw other pupils from my school walking like myself. It took me about thirty minutes to get to school which left me with fifteen minutes to find my classroom. I was proud of myself for finding my way and not giving up. Emma came to talk to me and I told her what had happened to me the previous day and I was actually surprised that she understood what I was saying. Maybe my English wasn't as bad as I thought it was. She told me that she usually walked to Ealing Broadway on days her parents didn't pick her up like today and that we could walk together if I liked. She knew a different way to get to Ealing Broadway which was quicker than the one I had taken today. Although we talked a lot especially during English class I didn't think she would be that friendly. Emma had helped me improve my English by telling me about her house, pet dog, family and then asking me questions about everything she had said the next day. I was surprised that I learned a lot from her and that I could have a conversation with her. As soon as the final bell went off to signal the end of school I waited for Emma by the big tree that stood outside the school building. After a couple of minutes she emerged from the tall, gloomy building and then we set out. The sight of the two of us walking side by side was on the funny side because we were exact opposites; Emma was tall and was even taller in her high heels as opposed to me who was not very tall at all. Emma also had long blond hair and I had dark hair which was not visible under my scarf. I guess what made it look bazaar was that Emma would hold my hand as if to make sure I didn't get lost! We used the shorter way she had been telling me about and within fifteen minutes we were there, outside Ealing Broadway Centre. We made a pact that from now on we would wait for each other by the big tree and then would walk together everyday.

The next morning I decided to try out Emma's route to see if I could find my way easily and to my surprise it was pretty straight forward. I began to always use that route because it was quick and very simple. At school I also made friends with some girls who were new in my class. I probably extended the hand of friendship because I knew how it felt to be new, alone and not able to speak English and I didn't want anyone to feel like that. My new friends were Zahada who was born here but brought up in Pakistan and Fardi who was Iranian. They were both very nice and happy that they had a friend like me who could help them when they needed it. We would go to the canteen together and remedial class and always tried to speak English to one another in order to improve. However there were occasions when we were left with no option than to speak Persian or Urdu because we couldn't explain ourselves. Even though I had loads of practice speaking to my friends and going to remedial class I wasn't very confident speaking English. It reassured me to know that I was not the only one in that position and that my friends also felt the same. I tried to keep improving myself by getting books from the library to read and also signing up to the mobile book bus which came to my area once a week. I would always get books to read and I would make sure I would complete them before I took them back. This was the only way I would improve my understanding and gain enough confidence to speak to others without feeling uncomfortable. Finally one day when I got home I found a bed in my room and mum had made it up for me. I knew that I would have to go to bed slightly earlier that night because it would probably be the best sleep I would have since we left the guest house. Mum and dad had one as well and now our house was beginning to take shape. The next morning was a hard morning for me to get out of bed because it felt like my bed was keeping me prisoner. Finally I tore myself away from it and got ready for school. The day passed quickly and when I got home I went and relaxed on my bed for a couple of minutes until I was awoken by a strange noise. I looked outside my bedroom window and saw 2 little eastern boys in our garden right by the front door, but from where I was standing I couldn't make out what they were doing. I rushed to the door and saw dirt seeping through the letter box slot. My instincts kept telling me to open the door, but then I froze until the dirt slowly trickled to a stop. Only until then did the adrenaline kick in and I rushed towards my bedroom window just in time to see the two little boys run out the garden leaving the gate swinging open.

They were probably of the age of about six and dressed in caps and normal track bottoms. So that's where the dirt was coming from. I couldn't believe it, why would anyone do this to another person? I had never seen such disrespect and such bad behaviour as I had just witnessed before my eyes. This never happened in Pakistan or Afghanistan because there children were taught to respect adults and others. I guess this was one of many differences that made me feel like I didn't belong. In my culture we always welcomed new people with open arms and helped them settle in but here it was the opposite, I felt like people weren't that welcoming. What had we done to these boys that they felt we deserved to have dirt put through our letter slots? I felt anger rising up me like a raging fire out of control. Quickly wasting no time I cleaned up the dirt and sat on my bed waiting for them to try their little stunt again but they never returned.

After a couple of days I returned home to find that the whole house had been carpeted. At last the cold draft that often found its way into the house would meet its competition. Walking around the house bear foot on the soft red carpet reminded me of my childhood in Afghanistan. This was perfect timing as winter seemed to become bitter. By now all the trees except the evergreens had no leaves on them making them look almost dead which made winter so dull and depressing. Mum and dad had managed to install a telephone now so at least now we could regularly keep in touch with our relatives all over the world. It always cheered me up to hear how some of my cousins and friends were getting on. I was happy because summer was drawing nearer and there had not been any snow fall so although it was cold it could have been worse. Spring came and the trees began to grow new leaves and the flower began to come out the ground. Some-times I would look outside and the sun would be shinning even though it was still cold but when I saw this I knew that soon it would be summer. Everything looked so beautiful, so fresh and I felt inspired. I was happy that winter was almost over; it had been a cold one for the locals so for me it was a very cold one. It would almost be a year since I started school and I felt that I had made progress. The weather began to improve and the days became longer as summer came. I never understood why the clocks went forward for summer and backwards for winter but I did it anyway. Having the sunshine coming through the lounge window made the room feel warm and bright.

Soon the summer holidays came and I made the most of my time by reading many books. I also tried to meet Fardi on a number of occasions and together we would read and help one another with our English. We became close probably because our culture was almost identical and because we shared a lot of common interests. Zahada on the other hand remained our friend but it was clear to see that we didn't share common interests because we wanted to improve our English through practising and reading, whereas she wanted to hang out with boys. She changed the way she dresses and started wearing short skirts and tight tops, this was a thing that was not accepted in my culture and I didn't think looked good. She also wore a lot of make-up which made her look like a naughty girl and this of course was a reputation that neither Fardi nor my-self needed. I was surprised because although

Zahada was born here she was raised in Pakistan and having lived there myself I thought that she would stick to her values and beliefs. What also surprised me was the short time it took her to change. Why did she want to change and be like the locals? Well I guess she wanted to fit in the way we all wanted to, but I wished she could realise that being yourself is sometimes the safest thing to do because it's natural. Don't get me wrong she still was our friend at school but outside school we didn't really meet up because our parents were strict. Half way through the holidays Fardi went on holiday to visit her family back in Iran so I was left alone for the rest of break. I was bored because I had read so many books and there was no one to discuss the books with. I also had no one to talk to in general even though mum and dad were around it wasn't the same as having Fardi here.

The holiday came to an end and school reopened in September after what seemed to be a long boring holiday. I must admit the best part of the holiday was the fact that the weather was bright and warm which made me feel good. When school opened I had now moved up to year eleven which was a very important year because major exams were done towards the end of the year. I knew I wasn't going to be ready for these exams because although my English was better it wasn't close to everyone else's standard. I also felt I would fit in more if I didn't wear my scarf to school. Although the holiday had been boring, like everyone else I dreaded going back to school but I knew it was just one of those things I had to do. The classes became a lot harder and I struggled to keep up with everyone and even though I didn't enjoy I still attended everyday.

Our teacher told us that we had to all do two weeks of work experience during this year. We would all get placed in a company by the school and we would have to work there. Even though I hated school I wasn't at all keen on this idea because I felt I would benefit more form coming to school for extra lessons but the teacher insisted that I had to do it and there was no way out of it. I reluctantly agreed hoping the ground would just open up and swallow me. I was told I would do my work experience at Boots Pharmacy not very far from home. I had to wear the uniform which was a shirt and a skirt which I didn't like at all because it was too short for my liking. I knew my parents would definitely hate it as well because the skirt reached my knees and for them that was too short. If I was to wear a skirt it should at least reach my ankles. I didn't wear my scarf to work either because I felt more confident with out it which was the opposite of when I was younger. I was also supposed to wear black shoes but I only had boots so I decided that they would do. The night before I was supposed to start I lay in bed tossing and turning thinking about the next day. What about if I made a mistake or what about if they didn't like me?

The next day I got up early determined not to be late on my first day. I made sure I had something to eat and changed into my uniform and set off. By now I knew my way around my area because often mum, dad and I would explore the area. I just took one bus to work and got there early. I felt uncomfortable and exposed in this short skirt but I knew I had to do this because my teacher's words rang in my mind. The manager was an elderly gentleman who smiled a lot and made me feel welcome. He showed me around and explained that they would try and rotate me around the store so I could do different things during the two weeks. I was first put at the photo processing desk where I was shown how to use the till, check for customer's orders and how to take an order. To begin with I was bored out of my mind and constantly glanced at the big red clock that hung on the wall opposite to my desk. For the first few customers I served I was so nervous that my palms became sweaty but after a couple of transactions I relaxed a little. I finished work and left at about 4pm and when I got home I was so tired. I told mum and dad about my day and they seemed pleased. I had my dinner and a hot bath which relaxed me. I sat in front of our new television and sipped on a cup of green tea. It was good to finally have received the TV because the evenings had been so boring but now at least we had some entertainment. Our home was slowly taking shape and this made me feel good. I almost fell asleep watching TV so I decided to go to bed so I would be ready for another hard day's work. The next day I rose early and got ready for work and left early to give myself enough time. Today I was going to remain at the photo processing desk which I didn't mind because I was now familiar with it. I still didn't like communicating with customers because I was shy and not confident and I worried I would not be able to answer their questions. Over the next couple of days I made sure I worked hard and if I didn't understand I always asked. After a few days I began to move around the shop doing various things rather than being stuck behind that counter the whole day. I filled the shelves with different products from shampoo to make up and whilst I did this I read the back of the packaging to find out what the product was for. Doing this actually helped improve my English and I would like to think it also improved my confidence because now if any customer was to approach me and ask for advice I knew what I was talking about. I was beginning to enjoy work experience here. The manager showed me how to do the inventory and I picked it up rather fast. I guess this is my strength, I am better at practical things than at other things. The process was very easy as it was all done with a small computerised device that was probably the size of my scientific calculator, then all the information was fed to the warehouse that delivered our stock. In addition to that I also had to print out a copy of the report and file it away in alphabetic order. I had always wondered why the alphabet was so important and now my question had been answered! Towards the end of the first week Tom the manager asked to speak to me so I stopped what I was doing and nodded. I didn't know what to expect, had I done something wrong? He then went on to say that I was doing a great job but I needed to change my shoes and wear flat shoes. I nodded and smiled but inside I swore at him. Was he joking or what? Did he really expect me to buy flat shoes just for the short time I was going to be here? As far as I was concerned I was here just for a couple more days then that was it and I was not crazy to go out and buy new shoes just to please him. So I made up my mind to take no action and continue as I had done up till now. Finally the weekend came and I relaxed my aching feet which were not used to standing the whole day. When I was massaging them I began to think about my past when we had to walk long distances and my feet hurt even more than they did now. I enjoyed the rest of my weekend watching TV and reading books. So this is how it felt like to work I thought. The thought kind of excited me because there was no homework to think about, no exams to worry about.

Monday morning I was back at work still wearing my boots and I continued with my daily routine. My teacher who preferred to be called by his first name, Steve was supposed to come see how I was doing today. I quite like Steve; actually I thought he was really sexy even though I never told anyone about my secret crush on the teacher. Steve was tall, well built, with thick black hair which was always cut short, and he had lovely black eyes that were full of peace. He came over and told me he was proud of me because even though I had been nervous about work experience I had persevered to achieve. He also went on to ask why I hadn't changed my shoes that the manager had asked me to and I told him I couldn't afford to buy a new pair of shoes just for the remaining four days I had left here. Steve smiled and told me I was right and that I shouldn't worry about it. By now I was able to help out customer's who needed help with certain products like the elderly woman who asked me about shampoo for dry hair. I was able to show her the products we did for dry hair all at different prices and she was very pleased I had taken time to help her out. Most of our customer's were very nice and I felt good helping them. I did have the occasional experience of the difficult customer. I was at the photo processing desk when my neighbour walked in and asked if her photos had come back. She didn't recognise me at all and I didn't say anything to her either. I looked for her photos and I couldn't find her and then I told her she should come back in the afternoon because we had not yet received them from the company who processed them for us. She wouldn't take my suggestion and went on to argue with me then finally she asked to speak to the manager. Tom came out and I explained to him that the photos had not returned yet and I had suggested she comes back later on after we receive our next delivery. Tom double checked to make sure I hadn't accidentally missed them whilst searching for them and found nothing. He told her to come back later and she began to shout that we had ruined her day and she had to come so far to pick them up as her home was so far. Finally after venting out all her anger she left and I told Tom that she had been lying about living so far away as she was my neighbour and my house was only ten minutes away. This made us both laugh and we continued working. Every day had been different and I had enjoyed all of them. Why had I made such a fuss about coming here? I guess it only goes to show that we are always scared of the unknown so we proceed with caution.

Friday came fast and I was sad because this was my last day here. I had begun to take a liking to this place and now it was time to leave. The day went by very fast and before I knew it was time to go home. Everyone I had worked with came round to give me a hug and say their farewells. They all told me that I had worked so hard and that they were going to miss me because I had become part of the family. I did feel like I was part of their family and I was going to miss this place. To my surprise they had got me a present and a card which made me feel special. I had only been with these people for a couple of days and here they were giving me a present. When I got home I showed mum and dad my present and card and they were so proud of me. I had done well and I had enjoyed the experience even though at first I had been so reluctant to try something new. The weekend went by fast and I looked forward to getting back to school so I could find out how my friends had got on. I saw Fardi and she told me that she hated her work experience and had left after two days as she had had enough. Zahada had also left just after three days because she too had hated it and so she stayed home for the rest of the time. During registration Steve told us that we had to write him a report to give him feedback about the people we worked with as well as the company. I couldn't wait to start because I had learnt so much and had enjoyed the experience. Our English teacher also asked us to write a report of about a thousand words about our experience and I couldn't wait to get going. Steve's report was only a short one because he wanted to know if we thought it was good so that they could get things ready for the next group of students next year. I was glad that even though the first couple of days I was scared I hadn't let this put me off as now at least I had lots to right about unlike my friends Zahada and Fardi who now spent days on end in the library trying to get information on their companies for their English assignment. We had two weeks to complete this and hand it in and I finished mine within a week. When I received it after it had been marked I was very happy because I had done well. I was also given feedback that Tom the manager at Boots had written about me. He had said that I was hard working, polite, good team worker, reliable and he went on to say that it would be a pleasure if I accepted their offer to come work for them on Saturdays. I was gob smacked because I didn't think I had made such an impression on him. Steve was smiling from ear to ear telling me that I had done well and he was proud. It just goes to show that if you put your mind to something you can achieve it. I couldn't wait to get home and show mum and dad my offer letter and my good grades I had achieved. I was going to take the Saturday job with Boots because then I could get more experience and I could start earning some money which I could use to buy some clothes. Dad was especially proud and when he hugged me I could feel how happy and proud he was of me. This was the most wonderful feeling in my life that I would never forget.

That night I couldn't get to sleep straight away because I kept thinking about my success earlier that day. This was what I needed but at the same time I wasn't sure because I felt I should spend more time reading and improving my English. This was my main priority because if I didn't improve my English what good would this job be to me? I didn't want to compromise my studies but at the same time this was a good opportunity for me to get on to the job ladder. When I got up the next morning I sat on my bed and looked outside my bedroom window. I had to take this opportunity I thought to myself but first I must put my school work first. I went and brushed my teeth, washed my face and had my cup of green tea still thinking of what to do then it hit me. I decided to first ask Mrs Khan if she would help me with my English so I could get ready for the exams and then later on I would take the Saturday job. That was the perfect answer that way I wasn't loosing out on the job and I would have enough time for my revision. Mrs Khan was more than happy to help me and we arranged our sessions for an hour everyday after school. So I informed Boots that I would be happy to take the job but only after two months and they were happy with that and so I began to have my after school session with Mrs Khan. Everyone at school was getting ready for the exams as they were approaching fast and I was doing my best to prepare too but I couldn't help feeling that I wasn't ready for them. I went to speak to my teacher and told him exactly how I felt. I wasn't confident enough to sit the exams and knew that even though I had been doing extra work I would still not be ready because my English was not good enough and hence I wouldn't pass. He told me that I was a good student and that he understood my concerns but he would have to talk this over with the Head-teacher. Later on that day he called me to his office and told me that the head-teacher had said that I was ready and had to sit the exams. When I heard this my heart sank to the floor and I felt like screaming because I knew I wasn't ready. 'No one knows you like you do,' that was a saying I had read in a book during summer holiday and I wanted to tell this man who was standing there telling me I was ready, because he doesn't know that for a fact or does he? I continued to try and work hard to strengthen my skills and when the exams came I was so worried. These were going to be my first major exams and all the pressure was on me, something I wasn't used to. My first exam was in the morning and my heart was racing, my palms sweating. I wished I would close my eyes and when I open them again my exam paper would be completed in front of me but of course this wasn't going to happen. I found this English exam very hard and I felt like crying because if they were all going to be like this I felt I had no chance. Those couple of weeks were the worst weeks of my school life as I found each exam as hard as the previous one. When they finally came to an end I began my Saturday job at Boots and the first few weeks I worried about the outcome of my exams but then I soon forgot about it, but then there was nothing I could change about them now. I enjoyed work and when payday finally came I felt rewarded for all my hard work. Torn between two sides, should I spend the money or should I send it home for my brother who needed it more than I did? Finally my conscious got the better of me and I decided to send it to him even though he had been so horrible to us in the past it was my responsibility as his sister to help him when he needed help. What would I buy with my first pay cheque I wondered? I began to work more days during the week as school was closed as we had done the final exams and now it was just a waiting process for the results which I was dreading.

That day finally came in the second week of August and as I held the envelope in my hands I wondered what the outcome would be. Had I passed or had I failed? I put the envelope away and decided to have a cup of tea first because my arms were shaking and if I could hold a hot cup of tea with out spilling it everywhere I would be able to open that envelope that held my fate in it. Finally I decided to open the envelope because although I wanted to finish my tea I couldn't taste anything. As I tore the envelope open my heart raced like an aeroplane roaring down the runway at full throttle. As I read the exam slip I felt tears building up in my eyes. These were not tears of happiness but tears of disappointment. I hadn't done well and I was upset, upset with my teacher because he hadn't listened to me now I was suffering the consequences. My heart felt heavy and I cried that whole day until my eyes went red and my pillow was wet. I felt my world had crumbled down all around me, what was I going to do now? I didn't even know what I would tell my parents. I was depressed for the next couple of days and so I stayed indoors allowing time to heal my wounds. After a couple of days I got out of bed and looked at myself in the mirror and remembered the promise I had made to myself 'I would never give up even when things didn't go right'. So with that I picked myself up and continued on with my journey. I remember how proud dad was when I received such good feedback from Boots and it felt good when he hugged me, I couldn't let him down now! It wasn't the end of the world so I decided to continue school and proceed to sixth-form. This time I promised myself that I would do well. I continued to work at Boots during the weekend which was good as I could still practise my English with my customers and I could also interact with my colleagues and this would help me with my English and my confidence. From that day onwards I promised to always do my best and to never let anyone put me down I was going to make it. I enrolled in an English course not too far from home so I could practise and learn whilst school was closed. The course was every morning for two hours. Sixth-form was due to start in September and I was comforted by the fact that I could choose what subjects I wanted to do.

When the holiday finally came to an end I decided that it was in my best interests to stop working at Boots so I could divert all my time to school. Sixth form was so different to high school because everyone dresses so well and looks after themselves. I remember thinking that these girls only came to school to show off their outfits because believe me it felt like they were competing with one another. I didn't understand it, what was the point of that? Everyone was so surprised that I didn't have my scarf on, actually they didn't recognise me until I spoke because during the exams I guess everyone had been so stressed they hadn't really noticed. So I was right, not wearing a scarf made me feel more confident and liberated. I was also right about giving up my week-end job because there was so much work to be done in sixth-form. From the first day I knew that sixth form would be a good experience and because I had my friends Zahada and Fardi it felt better to know that I was not alone, there was someone else going through the same experience as myself. I remember clearly the night I told mum and dad I hadn't passed my exams. Looking into their eyes I knew they understood that I had tried my best and they encouraged me to go onto sixth form and put this behind me by continuing to strive for a better life. I began to interact with other people more to improve my English. Every time we were given an assignment I practically lived in the library in order to read up a little more on the subject. Once doing the first draft I would ask the teacher to have a look at it and tell me if I was doing it correctly. By doing this it gave me confidence in myself and I passed that onto my friends who sometimes battled with some assignments. We would try help each other by proof reading the final copy for small errors that we may have missed and often I would learn something new from reading someone else's assignment. Once Mr Hayes gave us an assignment which I made sure I spent lots of time on because I found marketing interesting although it was one of the difficult modules in my course. When I handed in the final copy he graded me a merit and I felt like I had failed because the quality of the work I had produced was excellent even according to my piers. I made sure I went and spoke to him about why he had graded my work with such a low mark. After having investing so much time and effort into this assignment I was not about to let him just give me such a low mark as it would affect not only my grade average but my self esteem which I had spent so much time building up. He then read it again and admitted that it was an extremely good piece of work and that he would remark it and then award me with a distinction. I was over the moon because I had worked hard on that piece and knew it should be given a high mark. I saw less and less of Zahada who seemed to never be at school. Even when she was at school I guess because our interests had diverged we didn't see much of each other because I had made the decision to dedicate my time to school work and Zahada on the other hand was not very interested in school. She preferred to compete in the 'who can dress best contest,' and had become brain washed by the constant presence of boys at the school gate after school. Fardi continued to work hard to try achieve as well and together we helped one another. I won't try to deceive anyone, I found that year very hard because there was always an assignment or research to do. My English improved and I was able to have conversations with other students, teachers and this gave me the confidence I needed. Towards the end of the school year we had parent, student evening and I looked forward to this as I was now able to communicate with my teachers so hence I could find out where I needed to improve. Yacob attended the evening on my parent's behalf because he would be able to communicate with my teachers and then inform my parents of my progress. As we moved from one desk to another I could tell that

Yacob was surprised with all the excellent reviews I received from my teachers even though he remained silent. When we were finished he dropped me off at home and after an hour the phone rang and it was Zainab. She spoke to mum for about an hour and when mum was finished she spoke to dad who then called me to the lounge. I wondered what they wanted to talk to me about. I hadn't done anything wrong as far as I could remember. Dad started the conversation off by saying something along the lines of, 'I know how difficult it was for you to adjust when we first arrived.....' 'Okay,' I remember thinking, 'where is this conversation going to?' Dad smiled and congratulated me on how well I had done at school. Yacob had told Zainab about the excellent reviews I had received and apparently he had been very surprised at how well I had done. I could see how proud dad was of me and mum too and that made me feel on top of the world. I had always known that if I applied myself properly I would be able to achieve anything I wanted to. Fardi had done well too and she too deserved the success as she worked hard as well. As for Zahada I don't know how she did as I never saw her at school and neither Fardi nor myself knew what happened to her after we completed sixth form. Not knowing what to do with myself after sixth form I decided to take an English course just to maintain my English. On the first day of the course I was given a test and when they marked it I was told I would be put into level four as my English was good. I thought about it and told them I would be more comfortable in a level lower and so I began my English course. On some days the lecturer came in and on others he didn't, which made me very upset as it was wasting my time and preventing me from progressing. One good thing that probably came out of this extra time I regularly had on my hands was that I was able to think about what I wanted to do next.

I guess there where a number of options at my finger tips but I knew that I had to continue to study and so with that in mind I pushed ahead to try find a college. I came across a college that offered good subjects that were of interest to me and the course was only going to be a year after which I would be better qualified. As my first day approached I was nervous, I guess the thought of having to make new friends again and having to try fit in was what worried me the most. Would I be able to manage the work load? I got ready that morning and made my way to the college which was not too far from home, just a couple of minutes on the bus. The college was bigger than my former school but not as nice as I had expected. There were students standing in groups outside the gate enjoying each others company and I hoped in my heart that I would also be able to have friends and be happy as them. When I registered at reception I asked if I could do the foundation course but I was told that intermediate was the best option, because of my good performance review from my previous school. The first class was interesting and I made sure I took down notes so that I could go home and read them just in case I didn't fully understand something. I felt uncomfortable sitting amongst this room full of boys as there were only two other girls. This was very new to me as my previous school had been girls only and back at home you never really came in contact with young men who were not related to you. I enrolled in an evening maths class as an extra subject and when I got there I realised that one of the other girls who was in my class was there too. I so wanted to go over and introduce myself and sit next to her but then I just walked passed and sat on my own. She had chosen a good seat, right by the teacher's desk. The maths class seemed to drag on and I began to drift away. After the class I rushed home and had dinner whilst telling mum and dad all about my new college, what the first day had been like. I had a shower, went straight to sleep as I had had a very busy day. The next day at college as I walked passed the girl in my maths class she smiled and greeted me. I was happy as this was my first step to making friends and anyway she looked like a very nice girl. The day went by relatively fast. When maths class came I got the courage to go up to the girl and ask her what her name was. She told me it was Jamelia and invited me to sit with her. We didn't say much after that as we both tried to concentrate on the lecture. Over the next couple of days I sat next to her during maths class and she told me she was from Egypt. We only shared maths class as the rest of lectures were different. After I saw her a couple of times and we began to talk more, I think I upset her by asking her where she was from for the second time. I didn't mean to but it kind of slipped my mind, I'm sure she soon realised how forgetful I was at times. Every time I went to the maths class I would start sneezing and coughing probably because all the windows were locked and all the dust from the dirty orange carpet had no where to escape. The carpet was so dirty that I think even the cleaner was scared to come close to it. Jamelia on the other hand was fine, she had no problem even during winter when it was freezing as the room didn't have big radiators. Instead they would have a couple of small radiators that had absolutely no impact on the room. We sometimes were the only students in that class because everyone else couldn't be bothered to turn up. So there I was sitting in the classroom with tissue paper in one hand wiping the tears streaming down my cheeks and blowing my nose every few minutes. As soon as I would leave that classroom I was fine. One day I decided to skive my maths lecture and when Mr Stutt saw me in the hall way I told him that every time I entered the room I felt sick. Mr Stutt just laughed and let me off. As I was walking down the steps I felt so light, like a burden had been lifted off my shoulders. When I got to the canteen I turned round and saw my friend Essam running up to me out of breath with a huge smile on his face holding something in his hands that looked like my file. His face lit up and he laughed so hard and handed me my file, my pencil case, my books and my wallet. So that's why I felt like my bag had became lighter because everything had fallen out whilst I was walking down the stairs. I felt so embarrassed because everyone knew what had happened and they all had big smiles on their faces. I wished the ground would open up and swallow me as my face turned as red as a tomato as I tried not to make eye contact with anyone which would make me feel even smaller than I felt. By now I was laughing at myself in disbelief at how funny I had looked in front of everyone. I sat down and was too embarrassed to get up to go buy something to eat so asked Jamelia to get me something and she did. I knew that if I were to get up and drag myself to the front of the canteen I would start everyone off in laughter again. Once we had finished eating we quietly slipped out of the canteen to attend our next lecture and by the end of the day the whole college knew what had happened to me earlier. During Mr Stutt's lecture he asked me if I was okay now and everyone laughed. I knew he was referring to the events earlier that day, and I felt so embarrassed because everyone including the teachers knew about it. When I got home I told mum about what had happened and she laughed.

The next morning when I was leaving mum stood by the door with a big grin on her face and reminded me to make sure that my bag was closed properly. I had now got into the routine of walking to college every morning because I was overweight compared to when I first came to the UK. It would take me about half an hour but I didn't mind as I was getting exercise to become fit and healthy and at the same time I was saving the bus fare. That day was the same as every other day; we worked hard to try get all our work done. When I had free lectures I would go to the library and do research for my assignments, make notes for other lectures. I still had that drive in me, to do my best in everything. I knew that I had to put in extra time to achieve my dreams. Some days I would spend time in the library all by myself as Jamelia had classes, whilst other times we would sit together and help one another with the subjects that the other was weaker at. Sometimes we would have to get to college very early to use the computers because during college time there were lectures held in that room. On other days we would stay after college until it closed trying to type our assignments up to avoid disruption we would normally face during the day as teachers needed the computers for their lecturers. Jamelia and I became really good friends and we formed a strong bond because we were similar in a way as we both wanted to achieve our dreams. Everyone always wanted to get our notes because we always attended classes and made good notes, like Omar who was a very quiet student like myself, but he had a wild streak. I guess in society we always judge people on their looks not on their personality, and if everyone gave him a chance I'm sure they would see that he was just a normal person who needed a chance. One day he asked to borrow my assignment that I had scored distinction in and as it had been marked I thought why not give him a chance, maybe he wanted to compare my work to his. I was wrong, he took my work and copied it word for word only changing my name to his and unfortunately for him he got caught. He got into a lot of trouble and had to have a teacher to pupil appointment and he had to vow to attend every lecture from that day forth.

As I was job-less I asked my friend Asad who was working at a restaurant not too far away that I needed a job and he told me that they had vacancies. All I had to do was go to the restaurant and fill out an application form and then wait for an interview with the manager who would contact me after a couple of days to let me know the out-come of the interview. When I got to the restaurant I was given an application form by the manager who asked me to fill it in straight away and that I should wait a while and when the General Manager came in he would interview me straight away. The interview was not too long and as I sat there with sweaty palms I looked around and wondered what it would be like to work here. The time seemed to drag on as the manager continued to bombard me endless questions that made my palms sweatier than they were. He finally told me that I would hear from him in a couple of days whether I had been successful or not.

After a couple of days I received the long awaited call. Even though I had wanted to hear the outcome of my interview I now felt like putting that moment on pause to get myself ready for the news. The general manager Pete was very polite and when he told me that I had the job I felt like jumping up and screaming. We agreed that I would work on Friday, Saturday and Sunday evenings as during the week I had college. The first day I was due to start I was nervous as one is expected to be but I tried to remain calm. When I got there I was shown around and then I was introduced to someone who would 'look after me'. I learnt a lot that evening and made sure I worked hard because all eyes were on me. Unfortunately not everyone was as nice as I had hoped and for the first few shifts I struggled but knew quitting was not an option. I had never worked in catering and this was my chance to learn more and expand my horizons. After working a couple of shifts I got the hang of things and quickly began to make new friends and this made me feel better because now I had people I could ask for help if I didn't know something. I continued to work hard at college doing lots of research for my assignments and as time went on I noticed the reduced attendance in our lectures. I guess other people had decided to either drop out or maybe they knew it all so didn't have to attend college. I always thought I was lucky because mum and dad support me, helped and encouraged me and because I wanted to make them proud I made sure I worked hard. Some people are lucky to be given a chance at a new life and I kept this thought at the back of my mind, because I was lucky to be here. All the hard work paid off at the end of the year when I passed my B-Tec diploma.

On my way home one afternoon I noticed a big poster on the side of the bus stop advertising a new shop that would open up just around the corner from home. I had never heard of it but I had once been to that area as they used to hold the Sunday market there. I was curious and I guess it was an excuse to spend my hard earned cash. As I didn't have much to do that afternoon I thought I would just go have a look around this new store. When I got there I was memorised at the shear size of the building and the parking spaces. It was very beautiful and well structured and when I entered the building it was equally as beautiful inside. I was breath taken and intrigued at what it would be like to work in such a huge beautiful building. I don't know what led me to that thought but I found myself walking up to one of the sales staff and asking if they had any vacancies going. She showed me the large poster advertising the jobs then directed me to the manager who stood in front of the 'Refund Counter'. The manager was a tall well groomed gentleman who smiled at me and told me that they needed enthusiastic young people such as myself and that I should bring my C.V. the next day at four p.m. for an interview. I was surprised that he had invited me for an interview or maybe I was just lucky I thought!

The next day I returned, armed with my C.V. in one hand and my hopes in the other. When I arrived the manager was very busy merchandising stock and I hoped that I hadn't travelled in vain. After about ten minutes he came over and explained that he was very busy but that this meant that we would not have a normal interview but that I would go and help him with the stock and he would conduct an interview whilst I helped him. This seemed fair enough as I didn't want to go home knowing that I would still have to return on a latter date to do this interview. At least this way I would get the interview over and done with so that by the time I went home my palms would not be as sweaty as they were now. The manager was very friendly and he instructed me on what to do and I made sure I did exactly that following his instructions step by step. His interview style was relaxed and this made me loosen up a bit and as we worked he asked me general questions like, if I was at college and if I had worked before, basically all those interview style questions. After about an hour we were finished and he thanked me whilst shaking my hand and then told me that he was impressed with me and offered me the job. My heart beat faster and faster when I heard those words. He went on to say that I would have to have on-job-experience the following day just to see if I liked the job. I was excited even when he told me that I would have to start at seven in the morning.

The next morning I got ready earlier to make sure I was early. I got there only to find there was no one there except the security guards and cleaners. This made me nervous as my mind started to race; maybe I had heard wrong or maybe I was at the wrong entrance. After about twenty minutes the manager who I soon came to know him as Matt, arrived and apologised for being late. Other people began to arrive and soon there was a group of about twenty waiting for him to open the store. It took him about five minutes to do that and when we went inside the store he gave me a tour of the whole store. It was bigger than I thought it was and I also got a chance to go to the back of the store which was even bigger. The staff room was bigger that any other I had ever seen. I could tell that Matt was well liked by everyone because they would all greet him with a smile and chat to him. He introduced me to so many people that towards the end of the tour I couldn't even remember who I had met first. I then was shown what the job entailed. I made sure I worked hard and when I was not sure about something I asked. After about an hour Matt called me to the office where he asked me how I had got on. Time had flown by so fast and although I had been stuck doing the same thing for the last couple of hours I told him it was a good experience. He smiled and handed me a contract to read then sign after which I gave him my bank details. When I asked Matt when he wanted me to start he smiled and said, 'You can start right now if you want!' He told me that if I wanted to start today I should come back at 3p.m. I thanked him and left with a huge grin on my face. I went home and relaxed then left for work later on. When I arrived there the shop was completely different tot the shop I had left this morning. There were clothes everywhere like a tornado had just blown through it. I began to pick up clothes off the floor and re-pack the shelves properly. As this was a brand new shop the public had gone crazy at the large range of clothing available here and some how forgotten how to be civilised. There was only a hand-full of us because the shop was still recruiting staff as it had just opened up. I knew that it would take us a while to finish but we chatted as we worked. My colleges were very nice and this made time pass fast. I was supposed to finish at nine but because we had just too much work to do that we finally finished at about mid-night. I was so tired I could hardly stand up straight. I had never folded so many clothes before. I mastered the skill of balancing my two jobs and college very well but of course at a price, and in this case the price was not having enough time for myself or my family.

I continued to work hard and learnt a lot from my colleagues who helped me out when I wasn't sure of certain things. We all worked very well as a team and gradually I began to be given more responsibility which was a good challenge for me because I was the kind of person who always wanted to learn new things. As time went by members of my team who I had bonded with began to leave and I continued to take on more responsibility. Matt asked me to go on a management training course because he saw so much potential in me. I was proud of myself because I had achieved this all by myself and it made me even more determined to achieve my dreams. The management training was not too long; a lot of it was basically things that we came across during our everyday running of the shop. Gradually some of my colleagues began to leave including some of the managers and so I was asked to run the department. This was a big step for me as it allowed me to put everything I had learnt into practice and to show everyone that I had what it took to be a manager. Everyone supported me and it was a great experience. One day Matt came to my department to tell me that I had been asked to attend an interview for a Management position as I had performed well. When the interview came it went well as it was a one-to-one interview and it gave me a chance to ask questions. I received a letter a couple of days later inviting me to the next stage of interviews as I had been successful. I was so happy and excited but at the same time a little nervous. The big day finally came and I was anxious. I had to leave home rather early as the venue was all the way in North London.

When I got there I sat in the car and tried to gather my thoughts and pulled myself together. As I entered the reception area and looked around I noticed that I was the only non European in the room and this made me feel even more intermediated and my heart sank. Why would they employ me, I was so young compared to every one else and on top of that I was the only person of colour there. Compared to everyone else I didn't have as much experience as everyone and all the odds where against me. The interview begun with four ladies telling us about the management role and what was expected of us. They were all very well groomed, well dressed and very professional. The presentation lasted for about half an hour after which we were given a test which was a little hard. I was relieved when we had a break as this allowed us to have a cup of coffee, light refreshments and to speak to the one another. Everyone was friendly and this made me feel a little relaxed which was what I needed for the next part which was group work. We all worked well together and after that we each had personal interviews. By now I was relaxed and by the time my interview came I was calm and collected. At the back of my mind I told myself that it didn't matter if I didn't get the job, what mattered is that I had done well so far. I left at about 17.45 and on the way home I couldn't stop yawing as I was so tired. I got home and relaxed, it had been a long day. A couple of days later I received a letter from the head office and although I was anxious I was excited as well. My hands were sweaty and my heart beat faster as I opened the letter. What would its contents hold? I glanced quickly at the black typed writing on the white sheet of paper and as I skimmed over the writing until I saw the word 'Congratulations'. I was ecstatic, they had chosen me. I couldn't believe it, my heart felt as light as a butterfly. I then went on to read the letter in full. I had the job on one condition, that I move to where ever they needed a manager. They wanted to post me in a store in Somerset and once I read that I knew that unless they let me stay at my branch then I would have to decline the offer. When I went to work I spoke to Matt who congratulated me and listen to me as I told him that I couldn't move to Somerset. He gave me the number of the area manager who I could try to speak to about moving. When I rang her she told me the news I was dreading, I had to either take the job in Somerset or stay in the position I was in now. My heart sank, I had worked so hard and now I had no other choice but to remain as I was because there was no way mum and dad would agree to let me go to Somerset. I was very disappointed and after a couple of weeks I decided to leave my job there. I had worked so hard and it made me upset because the area manager had made no effort to help me after all the hard work I had done. I guess it was time to move on anyway as all my old friends had left and things weren't the same as the new people were not as friendly. I still had to attend college so Somerset was out even if by the miracle of God mum and dad had said yes.

I started to work at the restaurant full-time doing week-ends and evenings during the week. I continued with my hair dressing course which would take two years. I was on the second year and my teacher sent me to a placement at British Airways Campus centre where they did Cabin crew's hair. When I went there I was memorised by how beautiful it was and being around so many cabin crew I got chance to hear about the job. They all looked so beautiful and my heart desired to one day become Cabin crew for a prestigious airline. Everyone at the Campus centre was so helpful and nice to me. I started working there during Ramadan and when it was time for lunch everyone would put aside something for me so when it was time to break my fast I would have a collection of food ranging from crisps to chocolate to fruit. I wanted to get hands on experience of how to do hair but all I ended up doing the whole time was sweeping the floor. The stylist never let me actually watch and so I decided to leave. I asked my teacher if it would be possible to go to Tony and Guy for my work experience and she told me that they would never take me. She was very helpful and made a few calls anyway as she knew how much it meant to me. After a couple of days she told me that she had managed to obtain a placement for me at one of their shops on condition I went to an interview first. The interview was short and later that day my teacher told me that they had accepted me and that I would start next week.

I was anxious as I didn't know what to expect. Everyone was really nice and I felt welcomed. I worked hard and learnt a lot from everyone. The manager was so impressed that they wrote a letter to my teacher offering me a permanent position at their shop. The offer was to begin immediately but that would mean that I would have to leave my course and I knew I couldn't do that. This course was my safety net because if I was to take the job with them and then later decided it wasn't for me then I would not really have the full qualifications in black and white so with this in mind I decided to pass on their offer. I continued to work for them and go to college and after a couple of weeks they sent my teacher another letter giving her feedback about my time spent at the shop with them. They were so impressed and spoke very highly of me. She had never received such excellent feedback about any student before so she was so proud of me. I was happy because the job had been demanding because I was on my feet all day shampooing, conditioning and blow-drying clients. I continued to attend college and decided to increase my hours at the restaurant because soon college would be over and I needed to establish a career now. When college finished I worked at the restaurant five days a week. It was a hard job at times but this was the only way to get to the top. The more I worked the more experience I got and at the same time I made some friends who I spent time with after work. It was nice a nice feeling to work hard and then spend you money with your friends, I thought. On the other hand my parents weren't too impressed with my spending habits but I continued anyway because I guess at that time it felt good. As time went on I began to become a little more responsible and gradually cut down on the unnecessary spending. I also progressed in my career becoming a star trainer which was rewarding and then progressing to become a support manager.

My manager told me that there was another branch opening up not too far from our shop and that they wanted me to go and help open up the shop. I didn't really want to go because I was content with just carrying on with the daily routine I was so used to now.

Every Thursday when the local area meeting was held my manager was asked to convince me to join the new team because they needed me. Finally I gave in and moved to the new branch. It was exciting to think that I would be part of the team helping to open this new branch.

After a couple of months we had a big recruitment drive because we desperately needed new staff to deal with the booming business. One morning a young lady walked into the restaurant for an on-job experience day. We had had a couple of potential recruits over that week so I showed her around and told her what she needed to do. She seemed very shy but she worked hard. The next week she returned to start with us as a waitress and she continued working hard. She was very friendly and seemed to get along well with everyone. Her name was Naeemah which in Arabic means tranquillity. Naeemah had such soft brown eyes that were filled with innocence and I didn't know it then but she would play a big part in my life, in the years to come. We would talk about life and I realised that she looked to me as a role model. I wasn't looking for a friend but deep down I guess the thought of having someone at work in this new store who I could call my friend sounded good. Naeemah invited me out on several occasions and I kept taking a rain check until one day I finally agreed. So after work we went over to Spur and had dinner. We chatted about work and she told me that she looked up to me and that I needed to be careful what I said in front of a certain number of people. It appeared that some people we worked with didn't really like me because I was strict and because I ran a tight shift. We talked as we enjoyed dinner. Over the months we continued to talk and we seemed to get along really well. If I was short staffed then all I had to do was call her and she would come help me out. When ever we worked together we would make sure everything was organised and ready for the next shift.

One day Naeemah came to work with a smile on her face and told me she had joined the gym which was across the street. She invited me to come take a tour of it and enticed me to join by telling me what they offered. I knew that this was the start of a very beautiful friendship. So after work one afternoon I went over there with her and had a tour and I was perplexed. The gym was huge and had so many facilities like steamer, sauna, indoor swimming pool and it even had a gym just for women. It was very impressive and I loved it and immediately decided to join. So after work we would go to the gym and work out for a couple of hours before relaxing in the sauna. It made us feel so good and to add to our healthy regime we decided to eat healthy too. I guess it's always easier to do something like keeping healthy if you have a partner to help you during the difficult days and we enjoyed ourselves. Encouraging one another to keep going, we managed to loose some weight and we felt so motivated. Sometime after going to the gym we would drive to Windsor were we would take walks along the riverbank and talk about life and what we thought it had planned for us. I had never really liked to talk too much about my family, I guess I just felt that that part of my life was private but with Naeemah I felt comfortable. When we wanted to reward ourselves we would have ice-cream and sit on the grass in the warm sunshine and watch the ducks swimming in the canal. The flowers had blossomed, the birds were singing in the trees and the water glistened in the golden sunshine. I felt alive, motivated and wished I could pause this minute forever. We began to spend more time together and our friendship blossomed, and slowly I began to open up to Naeemah. That was a big surprised for me because I had never warmed up to someone so quickly but I guess she had a big heart that just sucked me right in. I knew she thought highly of me and soon she began to call me her sister. This made me feel proud because someone valued my opinion and looked up to me. I gave Naeemah advice when she needed it and it now felt like I had know her my whole life. She didn't expect anything from me and accepted me the way I was. I felt like I had known her my whole life and I knew she felt the same way about me. It was weird because unlike with other people we didn't have to pretend to be like we someone else or go with the flow, we were just ourselves and that was good enough.

We sometimes arranged evenings out with other friends from work which was always nice. Even more people began to interact with me, I guess they were intrigued about why Naeemah and I got along so well. At our favourite hang out which was Windsor we found this really nice Spanish restaurant that served lovely paella and we made sure we invited everyone to meet up for dinner. Windsor was a bit of a distance so when a huge group turned up I was so surprised. Everyone had a great time and we all got to know one another better. These outings became regular events; we would probably have about two a month which was always a task and a half to plan but loads of fun. Every outing was different sometimes we would go to the Spanish place, other times a Portuguese restaurant, and sometimes we would just be spontaneous and not make any specific plans on where to eat. Naeemah and I continued to talk and share things. For some reason I felt so comfortable around her and she with me and with this we both found that opening up to one another was almost magical. Naeemah knew like I did that when we talked the other would listen and not judge but offer advice. Up till now I had never disclosed where I came from not even to Naeemah, not because I was embarrassed but because my country had been ravaged by war and now been labelled as a country that 'harboured terrorists'. Like thousands of Muslims it was better to never disclose where you came from in case people took their anger out on you. She didn't push me to tell her but I sometimes hinted about what was going on in my country and I know she kind of knew. What was I afraid of? Did I think that if I told her and everyone else they would change their opinion on me? Maybe with everyone else but I knew that Naeemah liked me regardless of where I came from. Regardless I still found it hard to tell her. I guess what scared me the most was letting someone getting too close to me, that they know my every secret then one day they hurt me. Could Naeemah do that? She seemed so loving, so sweet and perfect, and there it was- I kept thinking 'if it seems too good to be true then it probably is!' I remember driving Naeemah home a number of times and when I got to her house she would turn and look me in the eyes, smile and tell me how special I was and that she loved me loads. I would always ask why she loved me and what I had done to deserve such unconditional love like I got from her. Up until today I have never been able to answer that question. We were always there for one another and supported each other. Naeemah was like the younger sister I never had and to her I was like the older sister she never had. So when we started calling each other 'my sister' it felt so natural like it had always been. In summer we would go to central London and shop until we dropped.

At work we had loads of fun as well. Naeemah and I tried to work the same shifts so that we could go to the gym after work or for a walk in Windsor Park. There were a number of friends who wished they could have such a strong bond as Naeemah and I had. We would work hard and when the restaurant closed we made sure everything was ready for the next morning Naeemah would help me with the paperwork whilst we talked. Winter came and time went by fast and then came the festive season of Christmas which always made the restaurant busy. Sometimes we were so busy that we barely had time to even look at the big clock that hung from the wall in the bar area. So when Christmas day came I was relieved as I had a chance to rest from the busy schedule we had had in the run up to Christmas. Two days after Christmas came the darkest day of my life. I remember it like it like it was yesterday and it still brings tears to my eyes and makes my emotions run wild. Naeemah and I were supposed to go to the gym that Sunday afternoon. I was supposed to ring her at about twelve and when I didn't call she got worried and rang me but I didn't pick up. Why? I was in pieces, I felt like a sword had been driven through my heart. I screamed, cried and felt like pulling out my hair. Why had this happened, why me, why today? Could we not have had another day? That morning we had all woken up to what seemed like a normal day, to a breakfast together when Dad complained that he was not feeling well. He didn't look too well so I got ready and took him to the hospital. So there we were Mum and I waiting for Dad to re-appear from the room he had disappeared into a few hours before but he never came out. I was getting anxious about what was taking them so long. After a couple of hours a doctor came out from the room and I could tell by the look on his face that he was the bearer of bad news. I remember everything so well right down to the very words that came out of the doctors mouth, "Unfortunately we did all we could but we were not able to save him......" and that's all I heard. Up until today I try to fill in the gaps of what came next but I can't remember. I was gripped with emotions and my heart was torn to shreds. I didn't have to even tell Mum what had happened because she already knew. Why? I was angry, I blamed myself, perhaps if I had brought him to the hospital earlier he would still be here with us. Just in a instance my beloved Dad had been taken away from us and we didn't even get a chance to say good-bye. I have never felt such pain as I did that day and I continue to relive this pain everyday when I think about him. Everything happened so fast I wished I could rewind time so I could at least tell him I love him always and that he was my tower of strength. I regret not having pushed to see my Dad for the last time just to say Good-bye to him as I knew him, even though I know his soul had left his body. You can never best describe grief, its one of those things that can only be explained by experience. We left the hospital and I knew I had to be strong for Mum who had just lost the one person she had shared so much with. I came home and the phone was ringing. When I picked it up it was Zainab calling to find out how Dad was. I tried to pull myself together but it didn't work and I cried to her that he was gone. She couldn't believe it, she cried and then spoke to mum. Zainab called around informing the rest of the family about the bad news and within minutes the phone was ringing non-stop. I had to make arrangements to fly home. It was frustrating to find flights at the travel agents because most of them were closed for the break and the earliest we could leave was the day after tomorrow. I was depressed and cried. My whole world had come crashing down into thousands of little pieces. Everywhere I looked I saw Dad, it was as if any minute now he would come walking through that front door, but that minute never came. I felt guilty, maybe if I had spent more time with him than at work then he would still be here. Time moved by so slowly and all I could do was sit and grieve for the man I loved so much.

Finally the day came for us to fly home and I wanted to get there quickly so I could be there at his burial. Maybe this was going to be my one chance to say good-bye. The flight was long and we had to stop over in Bahrain for four hours. I just sat and waited, staring holes into the air. I was glad I was not alone, at least Zainab, Yacob, Mum and my eldest brother were there. I was far away thinking of dad, where was he? I prayed he was safe and free from all the pain he had suffered all this time. We then left Bharain for Karachi, then after a couple of hours we left for Quetta. Up till now my journey had been absolute luxury compared to what faced us ahead. We were driven to Kandahar and the journey was long and exhausting. It was snowing as we drove towards Cheman from Quetta and the old car's windows didn't close properly so we all got really cold.

The car was very small and I found myself squashed in between mum and Zanaib as well as the luggage. There were no clear roads marked out and although I was scared and anxious about what the next couple of days held in store for us I knew I had to be strong for mum. How would I be able to get courage to go see my Dad's grave? Finally the journey came to an end when we arrived at midnight. I had had no sleep for the last couple of days and I was exhausted. The house was full of people and relatives who had come to grieve with us. We talked for a couple of hours and then at about three in the morning we slept for about two hours. Everyone had to get up early to have break-fast because soon we would have more guests. At about seven the first few guests came to the house to offer their condolences.

Guests continued to arrive through out the day up until about noon then we got ready to go see where they had put my Dad to rest. Everyone was dressed in black, the colour of mourning except my two sisters-in-law who looked like they were dressed for a wedding. This upset me a lot because it was as if they didn't respect us or my Dad by wearing bright coloured clothes, and all their gold. Dad had always treated them so well and told us to respect them too. When it was time for dinner he would call them to the table before us and if any of their children needed to be looked after we were told to do it whilst they finished dinner. This was how much he treasured them and they did this at his funeral. He had to be buried as soon as he arrived because that was what he wanted. When we arrived at the grave yard I couldn't believe that he was gone. I cried, screamed and hoped that I would wake up from this nightmare. How could he be gone? I was upset, how could Dad have left us like this? I wanted to dig him out of that dark, cold grave, hug and kiss him, whilst telling him that I loved him and that he was the best Dad ever. When he was alive Dad had decided that he wanted to be laid to rest next to his father and so we ensured that his wish was carried out. There was a Mosque near the grave-yard and so I decided to go pray for my Dad. I wanted to speak to him but I knew I couldn't so instead I prayed. I prayed that Allah would look after my Dad, set him free from all pain that he had endured whilst here on earth.

Everyday was different because we had different guests and although some things seemed routine it was just different. I couldn't believe I was here, back to where I grew up. Although this was not the same house I was born in I was home. Everything had changed thoroughly from out there in the streets to the people and even the house we called home. The whole set up of the house was very different to what I had left behind so many years ago and this confused me a lot. Almost everyday I went to Dad's grave because I felt this was the closet I could get to him. I kept asking him why he left us not realising that it was not his choice, then of course I would feel guilty for trying to blame him for something that was not his fault. I would just feel free and talk to him from my heart never forgetting to tell him how much I loved him. This was so hard for me because Dad and I had been so close that I felt so empty now. Every minute of everyday I thought about him and prayed for him. I was so depressed that I lost so much weight because I just didn't have the motivation to do anything apart from try to heal these deep wounds in my heart. How would I continue to live without my Dad, my guardian angel here to protect and give me advice? Life is so unfair you never know when the things you appreciate will be taken away from you leaving you as helpless as a baby. When families grieve you expect that every individual in that family knows what you are going through because they too are going through the same thing. I made sure that I hired the best people to build Dad's grave because he deserved the best always. So when I was about to leave I was surprised to receive a piece of paper from my brothers with a total of how much they had spent on buying food and basic commodities before we arrived. They expected me to pay up for everything. I was surprised and at the same time hurt. It would have been my pleasure to pay for everything because it was for Dad but at the same time being the youngest in the family I felt this was not right. He was my Dad as much as everyone else's. How dare they did this. I was very upset because they only carried out their roles as the oldest brothers when it came to selling Dad's land to give their families the best life, but here they were reduced from men to mice when it came to paying for funeral costs of their own father. Was I the only one who had realised that our Dad was gone? Was I the only one who couldn't put a price on my father's life? Time flew and soon it was time for me to return to London. Half of me wanted to just leave but the other half didn't because this is where I felt so close to Dad. I wished he could not see what was going on with in the family because it would tear him apart. I don't remember much of the journey back because I slept most of the way.

After forty days my body was so exhausted from the hard work, lack of sleep and probably because I wasn't eating well either. Zaniab and I both returned to London together. I came home to an empty, cold house and I felt so sad. Everything was the same as we had left it. My nephew and his wife were supposed to have come to check on the house but there was no sign that anyone had ever stepped one foot in the house. This made me so upset because we had looked after him so well and Dad had even paid for his wedding and I had bought his wife loads of clothes when she came to join him here. This was the thanks I got for looking after these people I had called my family. I just needed someone to talk to so I called Naeemah. She was so happy to speak to me. She said she had missed me and I could hear it in her voice. We talked, cried and she tried to cheer me up. There was so much I wanted to tell her and I knew that I would not be judged. We agreed to meet the next evening when I went over to see her at her house. After taking a shower I went to bed but kept tossing and turning until I finally drifted off to sleep. That was the first descent nights sleep I had had in over a month. I woke up to an empty house the next morning and I started the day by cleaning the house from top to bottom, then doing some grocery shopping as there was nothing in the house to eat. Zainab came over later to see how I was doing. When she arrived I made tea and we sat and talked. The conversation then moved on to what had happened between our brothers and I. I didn't really want to talk about it but she insisted so we talked. She went on to say that she knew I had some money that Dad left and that I should give it to her so that it is equally shared between everyone. I couldn't believe it, how could my older sister even think such a thing? I had bought everyone's airline tickets, paid 'the bill' that was forced upon me and paid for Dad's grave all by myself. Most of that money had gone towards the airline tickets and here she was putting such ideas across. That made my blood boil, firstly she had not contributed to anything and on top of that she had not even stood up for me when our brothers forced the bill on me. Family is supposed to be there for one another through tick and thin but here was my family ready to drop me in the fire. I felt so low by the time she left, but knew that I would have to keep going.

Evening came and I went over to Naeemah's house. When she opened the door I could see her fighting the tears of joy as well as sadness back. She gave me a huge hug and told me she had missed me so much. We sat down and had dinner whilst talking and she told me of how the days moved so slowly when I was not there. We caught up on what was going on at work whilst eating the delicious pasta she had made and Naeemah tried to cheer me up. It had been so long since I had seen her because I hadn't had a chance to see her before I left. I told her how hard it was walking up the path that led to the front door and when I went in the house how it felt like Dad was there. Naeemah sat next to me and it was like she knew how I felt because she hugged me as we both cried. She had never met my Dad but she grieved with me like she had lost her own too. For a couple of hours I felt free from all the hurt that I had experienced over the last couple of weeks. I knew that life would be difficult but Naeemah told me that everything will be okay and at that time that's what I needed to hear. I spent Sunday at home just relaxing and getting ready for work on Monday. I didn't look forward to going back to work because I just felt like being alone as far away from people, but at the same time maybe this was what I needed to take my mind off things. I knew I had to get back up there and continue my dream of achieving great things that I had always promised my Dad I would do. Up till today I think this keeps me going, unlike other people I will continue to fulfil the promise I made to him.

Everyone at work was very supportive and tried to cheer me up when I was down. Sometimes I would just go to the office and tears would stream down my checks because I missed Dad so much. It's such a horrible feeling to be surrounded by so many people but still feel so alone. After a couple of minutes someone would come to check up on me and bring me a coffee and that made me feel better. Everyone had been so nice and I appreciated that they cared about my welfare. They were work colleagues and many of them I had never really spoken to much but everyone made such an effort. Everyday was hard but having a good relationship with your work colleagues can make such a big difference. At last I saw how much people cared. I would always spend time listening to my colleagues when they needed to talk and I would listen and give advice to them. Now it was as if they were returning the favour by cheering me up and helping me. After work I didn't really feel like going to the gym as much so instead Naeemah and I would go to Windsor just to walk and talk.

I can't say that I was myself for a while because my mind was constantly on my Dad. I began to prepare for Mum's return by cleaning the house and doing the shopping. Everything had to be perfect because I knew that she had a lot more to deal with than worry about small issues. The day finally came when mum arrived and she was tired and I let her rest. We had loads of guests coming over to offer their sympathies. I had to stay strong for mum but looking at her made me feel so much pain. Here was this old lady who had just lost her life time companion and everywhere she looked there was something there that reminded her of him. I was content with supporting mum and being there for her. The first few days were difficult because mum would become depressed and that would upset me. The one thing that could make her happy I couldn't give her. Her health also deteriorated probably because she was depressed. The days gradually got better but occasionally I would find mum really upset and as a result I would get upset too. Work provided me with time to just not think about everything that was going on at home. I focused my energy on working hard to climb up the heiracy chain at work. My manager was very supportive and helped me with all the on job training. I continued to work hard and after a couple of months I became a deputy manager. I was happy because I had overcome so much. I wanted to continue to achieve my dreams as I had always promised Dad I would do that and now it seemed to be very important to fulfil this promise.

One day when I came home from work mum told me that a family who lived in America had called to ask her for my hand in marriage. I just smiled and dismissed the idea because I had so much on my mind at that time and really wasn't ready for marriage. Mum needed me and I felt that I owed it to Dad to look after her because he wasn't here to do that. Life continued as usual until mum told me again that the family called again. I didn't know what to say, I only hoped they would stop calling. My sister Elida called us that evening and asked to speak to me. She told me about the family and how wonderful they were and that the wanted me to marry their son. I told her I wasn't sure and she said I should think about it. The family continued calling and so did my Elida. She wanted to persuade me to marry but I felt it was too soon after loosing Dad to even think about marriage. I didn't want it to seem like I was abandoning mum. Who would look after her? I didn't know much about the family only that their family name was Tarzi and that they had moved to America before we had moved to London. They sent a photograph of their son who I was supposed to marry. Mum left the picture in an envelope on the table for me to look at but I wasn't really interested and it remained there for about a week until one day I decided to look at it. His name was Waled and when I saw his picture it meant nothing to me, the answer was still no. A couple of weeks later Mr Tarzi called mum and told her that they were coming over to Europe as they wanted to visit their relatives in Germany and that they would love to come over for a weekend to meet us. These people were very persistent and that scared me because they said that they would continue coming over until I agreed to marry their son. This was not the pressure I needed, I just wanted to be left alone to achieve my dreams and look after my mum. Elida kept trying to persuade me and at times I felt like she was pushing me into this. Yes in my culture young women get married without meeting their husbands and accepted it, but that was not me. I had now lived here for so long and although I was still very cultural I believed that a woman should be able to make up their own mind without feeling like they have to agree to please their family. Marriage is for life, a union between two people and I felt that in this day and age living abroad it is ideal to be compatible with one another. I was torn between two worlds on one hand standing up for what I believed in and on the other pleasing my family. I felt I had a duty to fulfil as an Afghan woman to do as my sisters had done but on the other hand I was not bound by the laws they had been because unlike them I had grown up elsewhere. I felt sorry for myself because either way I could not win. Naeemah told me that I didn't have to do anything I didn't want to, but it was easier said than done. She told me that she would support me regardless of what I decided to do. I was glad I had someone who I could talk to about all this, someone who was on my side. How could I please my family but at the same time do right by myself?

At work I continued to work hard blocking out everything that was happening at home. It was spring and the flowers were blossoming and the sun was out. Everything was lovely and I just wished I could just disappear into the wilderness. At night I would keep tossing and turning trying to come to terms with everything going on. What do I do? Do I agree and see all my dreams go down the drain or do I say no and 'bring shame upon my family?' I didn't want to disappoint anyone but at the same time I couldn't come up with a solution, I felt trapped. After a couple of sleepless nights the much dreaded news arrived- they were in Germany and Elida was coming over from Germany to help get everything organised for them. Everything felt so weird, why was I doing this? Mr and Mrs Tarzi arrived and stayed with Zainab. My heart kept beating faster and faster at the thought of what would happen that weekend. Elida continued to tell me that this was right, that I would be happy and so would everyone else. Samir called and told me that I should follow my heart, she would support me either way. For some time that made me feel as if everything would be alright but after sometime I guess reality would hit me. Why could everyone else not be as understanding as Samir? Everything was happening so fast and there was no time to clear my head. Naeemah and I went to get some gifts that I would have to present to my future in-laws and at that time I felt like I was dreaming and any moment now I would awake to my usual life. After that as we drove home I was scared, what was I getting myself into? I had no control over what was happening in my life and that scared me. As we approached the house there was Mr Tarzi standing in our garden admiring the beautiful flowers. I froze and then reality hit me. Could I bring myself to do this? I caught my breathe and squeezed Naeemah's hand to check if I was still alive and she squeezed back- Shit I wasn't dreaming and I wasn't going to wake up in a minute to my usual life. I felt as dead as a door knob, but what could I do, they were here and I couldn't change my mind now, could I? He left the garden and walked down the street, I hugged Naeemah tight and didn't want to let go. Finally I got the courage to go inside and walked straight through the house into the kitchen and sat there for a while and helped prepare dinner. I managed to stay hiding for the rest of the afternoon and when they left Mrs Tarzi came to the kitchen to see me. I wished I would disappear into thin air and as I stood there looking down wishing I was else where rather than standing here not knowing what to say. I was so shy and embarrassed especially seeing Zanaib had come over. They finally left and I felt relieved, but I knew that it would be worse tomorrow. That night like the rest of the week, I could not sleep. Could I marry this man? Finally I fell into deep sleep and my body relaxed. I woke up in the morning and first I felt like going back to sleep but then I realised what had happened the day before and a cold chill passed through my body. Suddenly my head was buzzing with thoughts, questions but no answers. I got up and help do the house work while Mum and Elida prepared the food for the day. After everything was done I took a shower and got ready. I heard mum and Elida talking about the Tarzi family and that the night before the daughter and son had arrived in London and would be coming over this afternoon. I could not believe my ears, everyone was making plans for me. They had already bought the chocolates we would have to present to the family to get engaged. It hit me then, everything was out of my hands, I had no choice in the matter. I felt upset and there was nothing I could do about it.

Later that day the door bell rang whilst I was in the kitchen and it was them! My heart beat faster and I felt like all the blood was rushing away from my face. They came in and made themselves comfortable and I remained in the kitchen the rest of the day. When it was time for dinner everyone got up to go to the bathroom to wash their hands for dinner. Elida invited them to wash their hands in the kitchen as there were too many people waiting to use the bathroom. This was the first time I caught a glimpse of him and his sister. Everything seemed to slow down and I could feel every second pass as the both entered the kitchen. His name was Waled and his sister's name was Leila. Leila was well dressed and smiled at me and asked why I was hiding in the kitchen. All I could do is try to smile but it was hard as I was so shy. Waled shook my hand whilst greeting me. I could not look at him so I looked down. As he left I quickly looked at him but he had exited the kitchen and all I saw was the back of his head. I felt absolutely nothing, I was just worried. This may seem like a silly question I guess, I was worried that what if these decisions people are making for me are not right for me? I had spent all my life moving from place to place and I didn't want to have to leave the place I now had come to know as home just because I had to move to America. How could I leave my mum by herself? This was my main concern because I felt I couldn't do that, She had just lost her husband and know I was going to abandon her. I needed her but most of all she needed me. After dinner everyone sat and made conversation whilst I sat in my room by myself straining my ears to hear what was going on in the other room. Elida gave Zanaib's husband Yacob 'the chocolates' and he passed them to Waled's father. My family cried because they wished my father could have been here and his family cried tears of joy. However I cried because I was upset, the dreams I had for my future were over and there was nothing I could do about it. Life is so unfair I thought. I had to pull myself together I thought, many people go through this and are happy. I dried my eyes but I was still very upset when there was a knock on my door. It was Leila, she gave me a hug and congratulated me on my engagement. She then returned to the lounge where everyone was talking and left me to myself. After a few hours everyone left and I helped mum and Elida clean up then we sat and watched TV whilst chatting.

The next morning was the big day and once again we got up and got everything ready for the guests that would arrive at about two in the afternoon. I got ready and Elida gave me special clothes to wear. They were green which symbolises Islam. I didn't want to do this and felt trapped. Everyone arrived and then at about four in the afternoon everyone had dinner. I kept out of site as usual and wished I could escape this trapped feeling. Maybe if I closed my eyes tight and wished hard enough it would happen. After dinner tea and sweets were served and the men left the room where the women were seated. The Imam started the nikah whilst I sat in my room in disbelief. Was I really here, was this really happening? The Imam continued to read verses from the Qur'an then Yacob's son came into my room to ask me thrice if I was willing to marry Waled. I had to repeat this phrase that basically translated to 'Yes'. Here I was saying yes to something I didn't want but I had no choice. My whole world fell apart and I felt so low. Other people feel happy and cry tears of joy but I felt like a load of weights had been placed on my shoulders. My heart sank and I knew that there was no going back. Why I asked myself? After the Imam finished the guests left, leaving behind Waled and his family, my family and my Aunt and Uncle. Elida came to my room and told me to come out and join everyone in the lounge. I was embarrassed and was hesitant but I knew I had to go. I stood next to Waled with my eyes looking down and my family took pictures of us. We sat down and I did not look at him, instead I sat close to the edge so that we had no physical contact. As Zanaib sat there watching my every movement, I didn't want to give her anything to talk about so I sat there looking at the floor for what felt like a life time just waiting for the chance to leave the room. I felt like I was on display, and with every minute that passed I could feel her continuous stare fixed on me. She was just waiting for me to look at Waled but I was one step ahead of her. No way was I going to give her the satisfaction. After a few minutes I left the room and went back to my room. I sat on my bed and questions filled my head, what had I just done? My life had just changed before my eyes, had I made the biggest mistake of my life? Would I later regret this decision? There was a knock on my door and Elida come into my room. She was so happy for me.

She said that it would be nice if we went out for a drive just her, Waled, Leila and I to get some fresh air. I got ready and then we left and the whole way to Windsor Waled talked about himself. He didn't give anyone a chance to say anything, I felt like he was trying to sell himself or that he thought very highly of himself. I tried to concentrated on my driving but I couldn't help thinking about what life with this man would be like that I got a little lost. I called Naeemah to ask her to meet us but she was a little shy I guess and felt we needed time to get to know each other so she gave a lame excuse. I now know that she wanted more than anything to be there and support me but she didn't want to interfere and thought it would be good for us to make the most of the little time we had to get time to speak and get to know each other. I decided to turn around and go to Uxbridge instead as I could never get lost. When we got there Leila and Elida got out of the car as Leila needed to smoke leaving Waled and I sitting in car together. Just the thought of how uncomfortable this felt he opened the door and excused himself as he had to use the bathroom, leaving me alone in the car. I felt relieved, I could breath, but I still felt uncomfortable. When everyone came back to the car I we drove home and when we got home Leila and Waled decided to spend the night at my house. Elida asked if anyone was hungry and Waled said he felt hungry so Elida told me to warm something for him. I looked at her and asked her to do it and she said that I should do it myself because he was my husband. That thought made me feel uncomfortable and so I just warmed up some food anyway and when he was done I washed the plates. He went to sleep and we sat and watched TV whist talking until the early hours of the morning.

The next day we woke up early even though I felt so tired I had to get up and get ready. We had breakfast then went to Southall because Leila wanted to get some things. The journey there was okay, everyone was talking and the atmosphere was slightly relaxed. We took the photos to be developed and after that we came home and sat for a while. I then had to drop Leila and Waled off at Zanaib's house and pick up his parents to take them to the airport . Yacob escorted me and when we got there we dropped them off as they were returning to Germany then proceed back to America. We returned to Zanaib's house to pick up Leila and Waled but this time Yacob didn't escort me. We got to the airport and Leila walked ahead of us probably as she thought she was giving us privacy. They checked in then she left us to say our good-byes. Waled looked into my eyes and said 'I love you!' I just looked at him as I couldn't bring myself to respond. How could I love him when I didn't know anything about him? Come on let me not kid myself, I had just met him two days ago and he was already telling me he loved me, oh please! I can't say I was it love at first site, but he was different, he was very well spoken and I guess compared to my sister's husbands this was a very strong quality. I kind of considered myself lucky as well because unlike my sisters who had got married without seeing their husbands I had had the chance to meet him before we got married. He gave me a small peck on the cheek and left.

The next day Elida and I went to the bank and then I received a call on my mobile, it was Waled. He told me he had got home safely and that he already missed me. In a way I was flattered but I also thought that it was so soon to miss someone, especially seeing we didn't even know each other but I guess that is men for you. There was a lot to do when we got home so we began to clean the house thoroughly. I was not happy and I guess Elida could tell as she kept telling me that I should be happy as he was educated, he came from a good family.....! How could she stand there and tell me all this? The family was invited for dinner at my Aunt's house and everyone was happy. Elida left after a few days to return to her family and my life kind of returned to normal except a phone call from Waled now and then. He would tell me about America and he kept pushing to arrange a date for the wedding celebration. I felt like he was the only in the relationship because he didn't ask me what I wanted or thought. He went ahead and booked the wedding celebration for 1st of January and now it was around July/ August. I didn't want to do this so quick as I needed time to sought myself out. I couldn't say anything and mum told me that it has been done so I shouldn't complain. It would have been wonderful to have the celebration in a big posh hotel like the Ritz Carlton with loads of guests but it was too soon. So now everyone knew that the wedding will take place on that date at the Ritz Carlton and mum began to prepare by making plans for a trip to Pakistan to buy stuff for the wedding. I began to buy things here as well even though I was still in disbelief I tried not to think about everything. I didn't feel like I was married at all and continue with my life. Waled continued to call and he would tell me about how everything was going with the plans. I felt a little disappointed because this man said he loved me but when we spoke over the phone it was always about him. He never asked me how I felt, what I wanted or even try to learn more about the woman he now called his wife? How could two people be married and the other not know much about their spouse? Sometimes I didn't feel like speaking to him as it would make me upset.

Then one day he called and suggested we cancel the wedding as it would be too cold in Washington to have the wedding and the guests would not come. I was furious, first of all because when I had told him to wait he went along and booked it anyway and now that everyone knew he has decided to cancel it. It didn't make sense to me, didn't he take all of this into consideration before? I put the phone down on him as I was very upset. He had made these plans and now I had already given my notice to my employer, what do I do now? After a few minutes Leila called and spoke to me and she told me that it was very cold at that time and tried to convince me. I just told her its fine because my opinion didn't really matter to them before so what could have changed now? After a few days he called me and suggested we rebook the celebration for March.

We agreed and then he went to book it. Before I got married I was in the process of buying a house and now the deal had come through and so as a result I had to work more hours to ensure I got a good mortgage deal. I called Waled and told him that I wouldn't be able to do celebration in March because I was tied down by this. I apologised and told him that this was a chance I had been waiting for, for a long time. As I had bought property before I knew that this was a long process and a good investment. He got upset but knew that if there was no bride there was no wedding celebration. He called me later on that week to inform me that he was struggling to try get his deposit back from the hotel and I felt bad as this was the second time he would loose his deposit. I didn't hear from him for two weeks so I decided to call him and see how he was doing. Mum decided to go to Pakistan anyway with my brothers and Samir leaving me at home by myself.

Whilst all this was happening I tried to take my mind off everything by concentrating on working. I would sometimes work for eighteen hours straight and not get enough sleep but it worked. On my days off Naeemah and I would spend the days relaxing at home talking about life. By now it was August and my birthday was coming up not that I remembered. I had been so stressed that Naeemah suggested that for my birthday we should go away on holiday so I could relax a bit. That sounded good and I couldn't wait. She suggested Dubai and we booked our holiday then proceeded to book the tickets. I was excited and so was Naeemah as we both knew that Dubai was a lovely country. Waled decided to come over for a week for my birthday and I could not say no because it would seem rude and he would begin to ask too many questions on why I didn't want him to come over. Mum said it was fine but we wanted to keep it quiet so that everyone else would not know. I told him to come the week of my birthday and so that his visit would not clash with our trip to paradise! I had to get everything ready for his arrival and I decided that we could not stay in this house so I booked a villa by the sea. Naeemah and I drove to White Cliff to have a look at the area. It was amazing and the view from the cliffs was breath taking. Naeemah would come with us and I hoped everything would go well.

The day came when he was supposed to arrive. It was about four in the morning when the phone rang. It was him telling me that there was a delay on his flight and he would be arriving the next day. I was relieved but at the say time worried because I wanted him to return on time so that we could go on holiday. I had to make excuses that I had three days training in Edinburgh for work so he could leave on time.

The next morning I picked him up at the airport and when we came home and I warmed something for him to eat. Whilst he was eating I began to put all the shopping that I had bought for our trip to White Cliff in the car as we would be there for a couple of days. I also made sure he called the airline to confirm his return date. As he had lost a day he decided to stay an extra day to make up for the time he had lost. I just prayed that there would be no hiccups and that he would leave on time so we could leave the following day after he left. We set off and picked Naeemah up. She would meet Waled for the first time and I was happy she would be there to support me. I knew that she would do her best to get along with him because we had discussed this a lot because she had been worried about the fact that what if they didn't get along. As we drove towards white cliff there was silence in the car and I kind of got a little worried. Naeemah had tried to initiate conversation in the car but Waled didn't respond as well as I would have liked him to. I hoped that the trip would not be like this, I hoped that he was not very talkative today because he was jet-lagged. We arrived at White Cliff at about 9pm and it was really dark as this was out in the country-side. We all got out of the car and didn't know how we would find our villa in the dark. Luckily Naeemah had a torch and whilst I stood there with Waled's arms wrapped around me she went to find the villa. I wanted to go with her but I couldn't get free. After a few minutes Naeemah came back, she had found the villa and the key that had been hidden under a flower pot. She had turned on the lights so we could find our way. We all went to have a look and I loved it as it had a unique design and it was so clean. Naeemah and I went to get the rest of the things out of the car as Waled had brought one of his bags and immediately went up stairs where the biggest room was. My mind went back to the day we were looking at the brochures with Naeemah and I immediately had said that I would have the room up-stairs but now that had changed. Why didn't he bother himself helping us bring everything to the house? I thought that was very bad of him being the man he should have help carry the big heavy boxes. Naeemah and I put everything away in the cupboard whilst Waled was upstairs lying on his bed. I made some tea and something small to eat and let him rest. I went to put stuff in the bathroom and when I came back to the kitchen Naeemah was there holding a birthday cake with lit candles and big smile on her face. Wow I remember thinking! What a nice surprise this was. I went upstairs to get Waled but he was already asleep so instead I came downstairs and I blew out my candles, made a wish and cut my cake. We had nice big slices with some tea whilst talking. It would have been nice if Waled was here with us but I guess he was tired. We sat and talked for until 2am then went to sleep as we were both tired.

The next morning we awoke to the sweet sounds of birds singing and the warm sunshine coming through the windows. Naeemah and I made breakfast then asked Waled to come and join us but he just asked for a class of orange juice as he was going for a run. So we got ready to go for a walk and waited for Waled to come back so that we could all go for a walk but he took longer than he had said he would. After patiently waiting we decided to go for our walk but we made sure that we left everything ready for him to have a shower and break-fast. We walked down to the beach and as we walked along the beach holding hands as we used to he ran passed and kept turning back to look at us. I though nothing of it and then Naeemah suggested we go back and let him have his breakfast then go for a walk together. I told Naeemah to relax, that I would go and get him and so I did. When I got to the villa he was lying on his bed and was a little upset with me. I asked him what was wrong he told me that I shouldn't be holding Naeemah's hand. I was laughing because I thought he was joking because

Naeemah was my sister and for us this was normal. When I realised he was not joking I didn't know what to say. I couldn't apologise because I hadn't done anything wrong and then I went down stairs to start making lunch when Naeemah returned. We began to make dinner so that it would be ready on time whilst he slept. We made sure everything was ready on the table and then sat down and waited for Waled to come down and join us for dinner. He eventually came down-stairs and we had dinner. Naeemah and I initiated conversations and tried to get him involved in the conversation. I kept filling his plate up with food so we could eat and relax a bit and he began to talk but just a bit. After dinner we did the dishes and made tea with my birthday cake which by now was half finished as we couldn't resist it. Waled said he was tired and went up stairs so I took him his cup of tea and cake so he could eat and then rest. Naeemah cleared up then went to her room and read her Qu'ran whilst waiting for me to return. I was upstairs with Waled, talking and when he fell asleep I went downstairs to see Naeemah. I kind of felt caught in the middle because at the same time I didn't want to make Waled feel left out but equally it would be wrong to do the same to Naeemah. I knew Naeemah was more understating and would not hold anything against me but still this thought stuck in my mind. Naeemah was in her room reading her Qu'ran and we talked for a while then I decided to join her so we could both read together. We went to my room and sat on the bed and read the Qu'ran, she would read one page then I would read the next page. I felt good reading the Qu'ran at the end of the day in such a beautiful place with my younger sister. After a couple of pages our eyes began to feel heavy so we both kissed the Qu'ran and switched off the light and tried to fall asleep. After a couple of minutes I was away in dream land until I felt something prodding my shoulder. I turned to my left and saw a dark silhouette of a man next to my bed, I jumped. To my relief it was just Waled. I followed him outside thinking that maybe he was hungry and wanted me to make something to eat for him but then he called me upstairs. I though he wasn't feeling well or had a problem with something and wanted me to assist him. To my surprise when we got upstairs and I looked at his face I could tell that he was upset. He began to tell me off for sleeping in the same bed as Naeemah. I couldn't take this anymore and told him up front that Naeemah was my sister and that we have always been this close and there was nothing to worry about. I was upset, who the hell was he to tell me what I can and couldn't do? I had known Naeemah forever and here we go, this guy falls into my life and expects me to cut all ties with my friends, I don't think so. He continued to shout and told me to go back downstairs to her room and sleep in there. I left and as I walked down the stairs he watched me and made sure I went to my room. I thought that Naeemah had slept through the whole thing but later on I realised she had heard everything. I was so upset and just jumped into bed and fell asleep. In the morning I got up went straight away to see Naeemah. I jumped into bed with her and spoke about what had happened the night before. I could tell that Naeemah was a little uneasy about everything that she had thought about leaving us and returning to London. I told her that there was no way I would let her do that, if she was going back to London then we all would. She was my sister and under no circumstances would I let this happen. Although the atmosphere was a little tense we decided to put everything behind us and enjoy the day. Naeemah made a delicious Spanish omelette for breakfast and we sat outside and enjoy our break-fast. Waled didn't come down for break-fast so I took him a glass of orange juice as I had done the day before. He went for a run and Naeemah and I went for a walk. The scenic view were breathe taking and I enjoyed every moment. We then walked along the narrow village street and picked up supplies from the post office. We returned and began to prepare dinner. I remember so clearly what we had as that was my favourite dish that Naeemah always made for me, salmon and pasta bake with a nice fresh salad and lovely warm tomato focaccia bread. I can still smell the freshly baked bread. That evening was our last evening there and we had dinner together. I stared a conversation about food and Naeemah joined in and to my surprise so did Waled. After such a long time he began to come out of his shell towards the end of our trip. I did the dishes and Naeemah helped dry whilst Waled sat on the stairs and continued to talk about food and cooking. After we finished Naeemah and I had earlier planned to go for a coffee at the local beach café, but when I asked her to get ready she suggested I go with Waled instead. We left Naeemah at the villa packing everything away, getting ready for our journey back to London.

Waled and I decided to go for a long walk instead and this gave us a chance to talk. He apologised for his behaviour the previous night and admitted that he had not taken the chance to get to know Naeemah, but after talking to her this evening he had realised that she was very nice. I accepted the apology but told him never to do that again. He began to talk about the wedding and what life would be like when we are together and what his plan was for us. After 2 hours we went back to the villa and found Naeemah in her room reading. I hadn't meant to leave her alone for so long but I knew that she didn't mind. We talked and then went to bed as we knew that tomorrow would be a long day.

We woke up early at about 7am and the weather had changed completely from sunny and beautiful to rainy and dull. We had a quick breakfast then began to check the cupboards to make sure we had taken all our belongings with us. Waled was still getting ready and so Naeemah and I took everything back to the car and went back to the villa for one last check. By now we were a little wet as it had been drizzling outside but that didn't bother us. We all left and Naeemah handed the keys in and settled the final bill. We began our journey to London early so that we could take him to show him popular tourist attractions in London. However the journey took slightly longer than expected as we got a little lost. We finally managed to find our way back to the tube station close to home where we left the car. We bought travel cards and our first stop was the London Eye and as we walked along the Thames river we watched different displays of music and magic shows. Our next stop was the Millennium bridge which we wanted to see as it had been in the papers recently, then finished off with lunch in a beautiful Italian restaurant in Leicester square. It had big opened windows which allowed a cool breezes to blow through and the tables were dressed in a clean white cloth with small vases of flowers. We ordered starters and main courses and to drink Naeemah and I shared a big bottle of cold mineral water and Waled had a glass of freshly squeezed orange juice. For dessert we went to Hagen Daz which had become our favourite hang out when

Naeemah and I were in London. Everyone ordered something different because it was a tradition of ours to always order different things so we could then share them so we did just that. We began our journey back and the tube was packed as it was now evening and everyone was going home. When we got back to the car Naeemah decided to take the tube home because she knew I was tired and wanted me to get some rest even though I insisted she told me to go home.

When we got home I made green tea for him and made his bed up. He would sleep in my bedroom and I would sleep in the lounge. We were so tired as the day had been long and my legs were painful that we both slept like babies. In the morning I made breakfast and he asked me to make him lunch so I made some rice, a green salad and chicken breasts. He then opened his suitcase and took out gifts he had brought for me, a few random perfumes that weren't in their original boxes and a cheap green ugly jacket which I, let alone my grandmother would wear. I was upset as he could have made a little more effort if he was going to give me something. I asked him where he had got the perfumes from and he remained silent which infuriated me even more. I didn't want to speak to him or spend anymore time with him so I had asked Naeemah to come over to pick him up and take him to Zanaib's house as they had found out he was in London. He was to tell her that he was here on official business and that he had only seen me at the airport and that is why Naeemah had brought him over to her house as I was busy at work. It was important that we did this as people would talk about us especially seeing mum was not around. He only spent about half an hour there and then Naeemah brought him back and left. We went out for dinner at a pasta restaurant in Ealing and when we got home I helped him pack his bags and he took a shower as he had an early flight in the morning. After that he went to bed while I tidied up a bit. In the morning I got up at 6 o'clock to make him breakfast and got ready to drop him off at the airport as he had an early flight. At the airport whilst I stood in the check in queue he went off to try upgrade his ticket to business class but soon came back because the queue was too long. He checked in and he told me that I should go to work and then straight home, I wasn't to go out at all, then we said our good-byes.

When I got home the house was in a mess and I began to clean up and washed all my clothes. I got out my suitcase and began to pack my clothes for the holiday which seemed to be the perfect answer. I was exhausted as I had been getting up early for the last week or so and had been cleaning the house and being the perfect host. I took a nice long relaxing bubble bath and made sure everything was ready for tomorrow. For the sixth time or more I spoke to Naeemah who too was so excited about our trip and we made plans about what time I would pick her up. Finally I went to bed and as soon as my head hit the freshly washed and ironed pillow case I was gone. Morning came and I was fast asleep when the phone woke me up. It was Naeemah, she asked if I was sleeping and I answered with a convincing 'No!' We spoke for a couple of minutes then I got out of bed and got ready, leaving the house deserted. I was filled with excitement as I threw my bag in the back and started my journey to pick Naeemah up. As I left home the car stopped dead in the middle of the road, and my heart beat fast. Was I going to miss my flight? I put my foot down hard on the accelerator and started the car. The engine cranked up and I revved the car and it sounded okay. I sighed heavily and continued with my journey. Finally I arrived at Naeemah's house and when she got into the car we were all smiles and the atmosphere was filled with excitement. We laughed and talked all the way to the airport and when we got there we checked in and proceeded to Duty Free area. The excitement was building up and we walked together to the aircraft. As we approached the boarding gate we were greeted by Qatar Airways staff who were well dressed. They boarded us and we proceeded to the aircraft. As we got nearer Naeemah felt for my hand and squeezed it hard, I squeezed back and we giggled like school girls. The crew greeted us with warm smiles and showed us to our seats. The aircraft was new and clean with loads of room to move around. As we settled in we watched other passengers board and observed the crew in action. Each time our eyes met we started laughing. Was this the same me, all thoughts of the previous days had suddenly disappeared and I felt alive and absolutely loved it. This was how I always visualised how my life would be. Here I was with my younger sister, my best friend enjoying life and not thinking about everything else, total bliss! The crew prepared for take-off and the captain greeted everyone and gave details about the flight. As we pushed back the crew screened the boring safety video but unlike all the others I have seen this one used 3 dimension cartoon characters and this just made us laugh. We were expecting the cabin crew to do their normal exit door routine which we loved to copy and take the piss out of but unfortunately it was all done by the video. We heard the engines roar as the captain opened the engines to full throttle and we began to charge down the runway until we felt the aircraft lift off the ground. Everything on the ground seemed to become smaller and smaller until we could not see anything but the white fluffy clouds. I pinch myself several times as I felt like I was dreaming. We were served a good meal and made friendly conversation with the gentleman sitting next to us. The atmosphere seemed so surreal, I was happy, we laughed and enjoyed our flight. Six hours or so later we landed at Doha International airport were we would transfer on to another aircraft. The first thing that hit me was the stifling heat that rose from the hot tarmac. I had expected a huge, beautiful airport but instead it was small with limited seating and a small duty free area. We had to wait for about two hours or so, so we used the opportunity to look around the small duty free area. It was finally time to bored our flight and soon everyone was on bored and we set off. The flight was very short and soon we landed at Dubai International Airport. My first impression was that it was bigger and better that Doha airport with such beautiful unique architecture. There were palm trees made out of gold within the terminal and leather seats for extra comfort, nothing compared to Heathrow where there were always old seats that you would never see vacant. We cleared immigration and collected our baggage then proceeded to the arrivals area where a hotel rep was holding our names on a board waiting for us to approach her. She took us to a brand new silver Mercedes and drove us to our hotel. As we drove we looked out the windows amazed at all the beautiful skyscrapers that were brightly lit up. Finally we drove towards our hotel which stood right next to the magnificent Burj al Arab which was and still is the symbol of Dubai. We were greeted by smiles as we pulled up to the hotel by the doorman. He welcomed us and took our luggage and when we entered the lobby area we were mesmerised by the beautiful deco. I particularly remember the beautiful flower arrangement that stood just close to the reception area and the sound of running water which ran from a small fountain into a pond that had a grand piano in the middle. This was absolutely beautiful and beyond that was the glass door that led to garden and beach outside. I had never seen anything like this before, but will always have that memory. Everyone was very friendly and welcoming, something that we in London were not accustomed to. Believe it or not I still believe that things as simple as that are enough to give you a buzz about life. Our room was spacious with a breath taking views of the beach and the Burj al Arab which was on a little island off the beach. Naeemah and I couldn't stop talking about the outstanding room and view. We were finally here together, at long last. Our lives we had left behind suddenly disappeared as we danced around pinching ourselves in disbelief. After we settled in we got ready for bed. As I lay in my bed that night I thanked Allah for bringing me this far, for giving me a younger sister who always had my back. I hoped that tomorrow would be a great day and that we would enjoy ourselves.

The next morning we got up and got ready for breakfast which was served buffet style. There were so many different types of food to choose from including continental breakfast using Hallal meat to fresh fruit. We experimented a bit and indulged in the sweet pastries that we only treated ourselves to once in a blue moon at home. After breakfast we went on a tour of all the hotel and got to go to the Burj Al Arab which was part of the hotel property. We went right to the top floor that was just a restaurant surrounded by glass windows allowing you the see so far across the sea. The view was so beautiful it just took my breath away as I had never imagined something so beautiful. We then went to another hotel on the property called the Mina Salam which was very different to the Burj and our hotel as it had a creek running through the grounds. The water was so clear you could see the bottom and there were old boats called dhows to take you across. This hotel also had a small shopping mall in its grounds that was just as beautiful as the hotel itself as it too was designed around Arabic architecture. The whole day we walked around and couldn't believe how beautiful everything was, even the gardens were full of flowers you never thought could survive in such a harsh climate. By the end of the evening we were so tired and hot we had to have a shower then we got ready and went for dinner at the Lebanese restaurant which up till today still remains as my favourite, Al Khayaal. We didn't know that the dress code was 'smart' as we were wearing trainers but they let us in anyway because we were staying at the hotel. We weren't really feeling hungry so we just had desert which was so filling and after which they brought us a big bowl of fresh fruits. There were so many different fruits some that I had seen before and some that I had never seen before .Everyone was so friendly and treated us like princesses always bringing us complimentary this and that. The restaurant also had live entertainment so we sat there listening to Arabic music and smoking apple shisha. We couldn't stop talking about everything we had done that day and the great service we had received. Everything about this restaurant was fabulous from the food, the atmosphere, the service to the cute musician. We finally left Al Khayaal at about 1am and when we got back to our room we went straight to sleep and this was the first night I really had a chance to sleep well after such a long time.

The next morning we arose feeling so relaxed and then we got ready for another adventurous day out there. Naeemah wanted to go on the desert safari but we thought we would leave it till the last day so instead we went shopping. We started off at City centre mall which was so big and had so many shops. We went all round the mall until our feet were sore then we went to different mall called Wafi City which is owned by Mr Al Fayad who ownes Harrods in London. This mall was so different from the shops that it housed which were all designer shops to its Egyptian architecture. It was beautiful and I made sure Naeemah took loads of pictures. There was so much to see there and I truly enjoyed it. The hotel bus picked us up from the shopping centre and took us back to the hotel where we freshened up and then went down stairs to our favourite restaurant to have a meal. We ordered and yet again everyone was so friendly towards us. We had our dinner and then ordered some desert and in addition they gave us a big bowel of fruits and tea whilst we smoked our Apple sisha. As usual everything was good, the live music, the atmosphere, the service. We finally tore ourselves from the restaurant and went back to our room and sat on the balcony enjoying the view of the Burj al Arab. It felt like a dream that I didn't want to be woken up from. We talked about our day and what we wanted to do the next day. We finally went to bed and slept well. The next morning we woke up, took a shower and got ready for the long day of sight seeing we had planned. We went downstairs for break-fast and as the day before we were spoilt for choice on what to have. I suggested we have a nice hot break-fast then we could move on to some pastries and finish off with a variety of fresh fruit as so we did that.

After we were done we went back to the room and got ready to go to a place called Karama which was supposed to be the Southall of Dubai! We wanted to see what it was like and because so many taxi drivers had told us that there was a market there where you could get good deals so we decided to check it out. To my surprise the streets were exactly like the streets of Southall only cleaner. As we got out of the taxi the heat from the hot tarmac hit us immediately and we rushes for the closest shelter. The shops were small and as we walked passed them young men tried to woe us into buying handbags. This would draw the attention of the shopkeepers in the next shop so they too would come out which made us both walk faster than we had been prior to this. I hated this idea of people trying to push me to buy something I didn't really want. Everyone was shouting, 'nice Gucci hand-bag madam, Versaci, Loui Verton, Burberry?' I felt like I was in an auction house where everyone was bidding for priceless art. I walked into a small shop with Naeemah following closely behind me and immediately the shop keeper tried to sell me something I didn't want. I felt like telling him to keep his suggestions to himself but before I could answer Naeemah had already declined his offer. We looked around a little more then made a quick exit to another shop what had drawn my attention by the beautiful garments they hung in the window. We entered a slightly bigger shop that had beautiful Indian garments and Persian rugs and a small Asian man greeted us. I wanted to get some beautiful pashmena scarves and knew from the moment I walked into that shop that this was the correct shop. The gentleman brought out so many different coloured scarves and laid them on the counter for me to choose. I picked a few and haggled for a good price as I knew that that was the key the get a good deal. After half an hour of haggling the shop keeper finally gave in and I walked out with a bag full of beautiful scarves. As we walked around I saw another shop that had selection of bed covers in the window so I went in. Almost immediately my eye caught this extravagant red and gold duvet cover. I would buy it now and keep it to take with me when I went to America. Even though I wasn't wearing my engagement ring this thought suddenly had managed to creep into my head. I stopped thinking about it and just made the purchase and we left the shop. On the way back to the hotel we enjoyed the cosmopolitan view and made friendly chit chat with the taxi driver. The traffic was a little bad as everyone was trying to get home for the siesta period but the taxi driver weaved his way in and out of the traffic and we finally found ourselves in front of the hotel. I was happy with the purchases I had made that day, as in London Pashmena scarves are so expensive and the duvet cover was very unique.

When we got to our room I put away the shopping a jumped on the bed. I wasn't tired but felt like relaxing for a bit but not inside so we decided to go to the beach as we hadn't had time before. I had never worn a swim suit anywhere else but the gym swimming pool. We put our clothes over our costumes and went to the beach. As the sun set behind the Burj Al Arab the water glistened like diamonds I felt like shouting 'Allah Akbar' because the view was so beautiful. We put our belongings on the beach beds and went into the water which was nice and warm. We played around in the water and then went and sat on our beach beds. I sat there playing with the sand like a small child on her first visit to the beach. Naeemah laughed and took loads of pictures and up till today she has never let me forget it! There was a cool breeze and we sat there admiring the view which seemed to drown out the noise from the children who were playing around in the water. As the sun set we decided to go for a walk in the hotel gardens which up until now we had only seen from our room balcony. The swimming pool was as blue as the sky and made you feel like jumping in. The gardens were full of exotic flowers of all colours that smelt so sweet and looking at the green grass one would never imagine that this lush green grass could grow so well in this harsh climate but there it was beneath my toes. The gardens was well lit and had beautiful monuments as well as cascading water features. We went up to our room in the glass lift which allowed us to look out over the gardens towards the Burj al Arab and the beach which was breath-taking. I took a shower as I had salt in my hair and sand all over my legs then got ready to go for dinner.

We decided to try something different so we went to another restaurant. We left and took a lift to the lobby and I couldn't help admire myself in the glass mirrors of the lift. When we got to the ground floor the doors opened and Naeemah shouted at me to hurry up as she was hungry. She told me to hurry up but I teased her and started dancing then suddenly the lift door began to close. I scurried for the door shouting at it as if it would listen to me and suddenly obey my commands to open up again. Naeemah too scurried across to try force the door open and hit the open button but the door continued to close. She stood there with a huge grin on her face as if to say ' I told you so!' I couldn't help but laugh at what had just happened. The lift took me up to the very top floor where a young father and his family got into the lift then we proceeded down again stopping along the way to pick up an elderly couple. When the lift doors finally opened up on the ground floor there stood Naeemah laughing her lungs out. As soon as I saw her I too burst into laughter and everyone in the lifts looked at us like we had just escaped from a mental asylum. We laughed until our ribs became painful and tears ran down our cheeks.

The meal was very different from the Lebanese restaurant but we thoroughly enjoyed it. The restaurant served a buffet dinner with a delicious variety which made me confused as I didn't know what to have. After careful consideration we chose to have a main meal and dessert rather than a starter, main meal and desert as we would definitely not finish. The meal was delicious and the best word to describe the dessert is -heavenly! After dinner we sat there stuffed to the brim talking about what we would do the following day. We admired the good-looking gentlemen who were walking around and chatted a little more. Our holiday in paradise had almost come to an end but I had had the best time of my life with the best company I could have imagined. I had to go to use the bathroom and as I was in my own little world I just walked into the bathroom and as I came out to wash my hands I saw two Arabic men wearing white robes standing by the urinals taking a leak. Oh my gosh, I hadn't realised but I had gone into the gents bathroom! Luckily they had not seen me so I quickly went back into the cubicle but just when I thought I might get away with this a handyman walked into the bathroom to change some light bulbs. He stood on a tall ladder and as he was changing the bulb he saw me standing in the cubicle. Only God knows what went through his mind! How would I get out without the other men seeing me? I didn't want them to think I had done this on purpose. They would have to leave soon so I waited and as soon as they left I left the cubicle and darted out across the hallway to the ladies to wash my hands. When Naeemah saw the big grin on my face she knew something had happened and when I told her we laughed so much. I was happy that I had made it out without anyone seeing me. To date every time I say to her that I am going to use the bathroom Naeemah always reminds me to make sure I use the ladies not the men's! We sat talking about life until the early hours of the morning then we went to our room. I lay there staring at the ceiling thinking about what such a good time I had had here and how things would change soon as I was married. I had had so much freedom and couldn't see myself giving it all up. I knew Waled was nice and that he loved me but that was he the man for me? Well even though I felt this way was there any other solution but to just marry him? All that thinking gave me a head-ache so I got out of bed and went out to the balcony to get some fresh air. Would this be the last time I would be able to visit Dubai and thoroughly enjoy myself or was I just dreaming? How would life be when I was married, would I enjoy all this freedom or would I be sentenced to prison, not being able to leave my husband's side without his permission? The sea and land seemed to speak to me and win me over and it is with this I made a promise that I would be back, married or not, no one would stop me.

The next morning I got up and a smile came to my face when I remembered where I was then as quickly as it came it went when I remembered that today was the last day I would be here in paradise. We got ready and went downstairs for breakfast. This was our last breakfast here in Dubai and we felt a little sad because it had all come to an end. We enjoyed the breakfast and then went back to the room to pack our bags ready for check out. The luggage would have to be left with the concierge until we returned later on that afternoon as our flight was only in the evening. We would have to spend the day waiting around so we checked out at the latest possible time which was twelve o'clock then we went to the lobby area where we settled up our bill and decided to go to a shopping mall for a few hours. We didn't really have much money to spend but we still had a good time then returned to the hotel at about four in the afternoon. To capture this special holiday we took loads of photos that afternoon so that we would always have a photographic memory of how beautiful everything was. My stomach started to voice it's hunger pains so I suggested that we should get something to eat before heading off to the airport so we decided to eat at a restaurant at the hotel that had tables outside as well as inside. We decided to take advantage of the last few hours we had here so we sat outside in the humid air and we ordered some Arabic rice, lamb with a salad. I didn't expect anything less than the high quality of the food I had experienced at the hotel so far. We ate until we could not manage anymore then we sat and enjoyed the atmosphere whilst smoking apple shisha and talked. After a while I asked for the bill then decided it was time to go, after all we didn't want to miss our flight.

We took a taxi to the airport and by now I was really feeling tired and easily agitated. Naeemah was in good spirits as usual and praised me for haggling to get good deals for everything we bought. I don't know why exactly why I snapped at her but I did, probably because I felt the taxi driver was staring at me with his judgemental eyes. After that the mood in the taxi changed like that and we stopped talking and I just looked out of the taxi window at all the beautiful buildings. I felt like she was making fun of me and my haggling method showing me up in front of him. I know she had no intention of doing that but at that time that's how it felt. I later found out that she had been complementing me because if I hadn't haggled prices we would have been like many other tourists, ripped off. She didn't think the taxi driver was listening or that he was at all interested because he was so busy listening to his Indian music that blasted out the radio. Even if he was ease dropping he wouldn't have a clue what we were talking about and if he did then he would know that that was perfectly normal in Dubai, for people to haggle. I guess I was tired and probably annoyed at having to go back to my old life that I dreaded but couldn't escape. Naeemah apologised profusely but I just didn't want to hear it because as far as I was concerned I was right. Naeemah knew me very well and I that is probably why she always knew what to do when we had an argument and she did just that. We checked in and proceeded to the duty free area where we saw many people taking full advantage of the duty free bargains like this Asian man who had bought so much tobacco he could not zip up his bag and so in order to close his bag he had to stand on it and his friend help him. That was something you never saw at Heathrow. I looked around a bit then decided to go to the gate and wait for boarding, I was not looking forward to the flight back home. We sat there and I began to try talk to Naeemah, I didn't want to spoil this lovely holiday by leaving with tension between us. We began boarding and when we got to our seats as usual Naeemah let me have the window seat and she sat in the middle. This small gesture made me feel good and it show me how much she loved me, no matter what I had reacted and with that I forgot about the earlier squabble. The flight was short and as soon as we had boarded we found ourselves disembarking the aircraft at Doha international airport. The airport seemed worse at night, gloomy and dull than it did when we were going to Dubai. This airport was nothing compared to the prestigious and beautiful airport in Dubai. I went towards the small duty free shop we had passed through on our way to Dubai to see if I could pick up some spices that had caught my eye on my last visit. There were so many spices, from cinnamon, nutmeg, saffron that it was so easy to find everything I needed and the plus side was that it was so cheap. We looked around until something caught my eye in the jewellery section. I walked quickly to look at the gold that glistened under the bright display lights and I began to talk to the lady behind the counter whilst trying on the jewellery. A beautiful ring caught my eye and when I tried it on it fitted perfectly until I looked at how expensive it was. After admiring more jewellery pieces we decided to go have a cup of coffee as we had a long wait install. There was a small coffee shop tucked away in the far corner of the airport, behind all the construction work that once completed would probably ensure more duty free shops and cafes. The coffee shop was full of people all of different origins and once we found a table I had a look at their menu. A young man came over to take our order and after 10minutes or so he brought our coffee over. Normally I drink black coffee and enjoy it but when I put the mug towards my mouth I could smell the extremely strong coffee scent. When I looked into the mug of coffee it looked like black hot tar. I added some milk to it and even though I had almost emptied the jug of milk into my mug it was still far to strong to drink. I took a small sip and immediately put the mug down and screwed my face to the revolting taste. We called the young man over and told him that the coffee was inconsumable and he didn't even apologise he just took the mugs away. Naeemah suggested we leave because she was always weary of disgruntled waiters who spit into customers drinks to 'teach them a lesson.' We walked around trying to find somewhere to sit and wait but everywhere we went was full of people. I really needed to use the toilet and so when we went passed one I quickly suggested Naeemah go in first to check it out. She gladly went and after a few minutes she came back with a disgusted look on her face. The toilets were not very clean and smelt very bad as the air conditioning unit was not working so the air was stagnant so the stale smell of urine lingered in the air. I hesitated then went in whilst Naeemah waited outside for me. When I came out Naeemah's checks were as red as fresh cherries and she had a big smile on her face. I didn't even have to ask when I saw this young gentleman walk passed and gave us a smile that made us melt in our shoes. I looked at Naeemah and she told me all about this group of young gorgeous sports men who were in the terminal and a group of them had walked by whilst I was in the terminal. Oh it was so exciting I felt 19 again! We walked further until we found somewhere to sit down and began our long wait. I observed the people sitting around us, they were mostly families or mothers travelling with children. There were prayer rooms to our right one for ladies and the other for men. The area we sat in was not too bad it had comfortable seating, was fairly clean and had a few television monitors showing the status of flights. As we sat there looking around we began to talk about how many hours we had left before we would be on our way home. We still had about 3 hours to go so we did as everyone else and got comfortable until this gentleman started snoring and I had to laugh. I didn't even have to say anything to Naeemah she had already read my mind and we both laughed quietly, careful not to wake him up. He sat there in deep sleep with his head tilted back and his mouth wide open snoring. A couple of minutes later the joke was over and we returned to glancing at the information screen and talking as time dragged by.

After what seemed to be eternity the flight was assigned a gate and we then proceeded towards the gate where boarding would begin in about 30 minutes. Finally boarding commenced and when we got on board we realised that the gentleman who had checked us in had made a mistake and not given us the window seat we had requested. I was so tired so we just sat in the seats we were assigned which were not too bad, an aisle and the one next to it in the middle. Once everyone was onboard the safety video was screened and the aircraft pushed back. Soon we were airborne and dinner was served which we both enjoyed as it was lamb. We got comfortable and tried to sleep. The crew were not as nice as the crew who had taken us out and we realised when I asked for another blanket as it was cold. Anyway everyone settled and the lights were dimmed until the morning when breakfast was served. We touched down to a wet, dull, windy London and we disembarked and headed straight for immigration as we knew it would be very full as it was peak time in the airport. The queue for other passport holders which Naeemah was supposed to join was so long that I could not let her join that queue so I decided to take things into my own hands. Without wasting anymore time I approached the gentleman who was monitoring the queue and told him that I couldn't leave my younger sister in the other queue as she may get lost and I didn't want to get in trouble with our parents if that happened. He was very nice and let us both go into the shorter queue but warned that if we were sent back we would have to join the back of the long queue. When we got to the immigration desk the gentleman smiled, stamped our passports and said ' Welcome Home!' We went down to the baggage reclaim hall and picked up our bags and proceeded home. That day I rested and I made sure I did my laundry, cleaned the house and when I spoke to Naeemah later on that evening although we had just spent five days together we had so much to talk about.

For the next week I rested at home and then returned to work. I was at home on my own as mum had not yet returned. Waled had called so many times whilst I was away and left so many messages so every time the phone rang I dreaded picking it up as it might be him and I knew he would go on and on about this. He also called Zanaib's house to find out where I was. He called to speak to me and I didn't really want to speak to him but at the same time didn't want to be rude. Sometimes I would look at my cousins who had got engaged with out seeing their husband or wife and yet they were happy or let's say they appeared to be happy. He would tell me that he looked forward to being with me and that he loved me and I felt sorry for him because I didn't feel anything for him. I thought it was preposterous for him to profess his love for me when he didn't know me. How can you love someone you don't know? I would just listen to everything he would say and after that I would feel sick to the stomach because I didn't love this man and I couldn't see myself living with him as there was no attraction. He would continue talking about how great he was and how lovely his house was, blabbla.... I felt like putting the phone on the side and continue watching television until he was finished because I didn't care about his house, his job. My ideal picture of 'when a man loves a woman' he would ask about her, about her day, her job, her life. Most of the time we would end up fighting, with me telling him to find someone else as we were far too different and he was expecting too much of me as I couldn't turn my feelings for him as he would like me too. I guess this was how my culture worked two people who didn't know anything about one another were expected to get married, start a family and live happily ever after. Like everyone else I guess I would have to learn to love him with time. My mum would always tell me that that we would learn to love and learn about each other once we start living together.

Mum finally returned with loads of suitcases filled with clothes, gold jewellery, materials, scarves all in preparation for 'my wedding' , the wedding that everyone else wanted but me. After we had been back a few weeks we decided to go out for dinner in an Arabic area, Edgware Road to relive our holiday. There were so many different restaurants to choose from but we finally found one that had a big television screen on the wall with Arabic music videos playing which made the atmosphere very lively. The deco was very Arabic with beautiful domes and gold furnishings. We were shown to our table which was right in the centre of the restaurant. The table was very small but we didn't mind. We ordered our main meal and then had some tea and Baklava for desert accompanied with shisha. While we sat there talking away, this young gentleman who was sitting two tables away kept staring at me. He was very good looking but I wasn't sure if he was looking at me or if he was looking at the large TV screen. I told Naeemah not to make it obvious when I told her that he was staring. After she did her best to not make it obvious she looked over in his direction and agreed instantly. We continued talking and he continued staring and I kept watching him stare. Naeemah went up to the bathroom and when she came back I asked her to settle the bill so we could leave. We left the money on the table and walked out. We had had a great time and when we got outside I turned around and saw him running towards me. I stopped and walked back to him, he was so tall, fair and handsome. He stretched out his hand and shook my hand introducing himself as Vim. He took my phone number and said he wanted to get to know us. We left and on the way home we talked about this mysterious man. Just as Naeemah was about to drop me off at home I received a text message from Vim saying how nice it was to meet me and that made my heart skip a beat. I was flattered that this gorgeous young man thought I was lovely and had taken an interest to me. Why couldn't this be the man I was to spend the rest of my life with? It was well after midnight now and we said our good-byes and I went home.

The following day was just like any other day until I received another text message asking us to meet up with him on Tuesday. I called Naeemah and she said that was okay and so we decided to meet at the same restaurant. I couldn't wait and Naeemah seemed excited too probably because she knew she would have company too, shisha. So on Tuesday we got ready and I picked Naeemah up and we were on our way to Edgware Road. He was already there waiting for us and he introduced himself again. We sat down and introduced ourselves again and made small chit-chat. The waiter came and took our orders and he asked what we did and where were originally from? I found out that he was Indian which was a big shock because when I first saw him I thought he was Arabic as he was so fair but I was wrong. He was studying to be a lawyer and had big ambitions. He was such a gentleman and had a great sense of humour. I guess the thing that really drew me to him was the fact that he made me feel special by asking about me, treating me like a princess, something I obviously didn't get from Waled. Vim was lovely but I knew I was a married woman and that this would only work if we remained just friends. He always knew the right things to say and that made me feel good about life. We had dinner and Naeemah and I shared the shisha as usual whilst talking to him. After a few hours we paid the bill and left. He walked us to the car and bade us good-bye. I had had a great time and so had Naeemah, she thought he was nice. She like the fact that he was very friendly speaking to both of us and she didn't feel left out at all. Naeemah was very sociable until she met Waled, because after everything that had happened when he came here she was a little hesitant. I guess it was because before she met him she had already made up her mind that she had to do her best to get along with him because after all this was going to be her brother-in-law but unfortunately after the way he behaved she felt she had failed.

The next couple of weeks were exciting as I continued to get more text messages from Vim. We all met up again during Ramadan and although he was not Muslim he respected the religion and when we broke our fast then he ate as well. We enjoyed dinner, tea and shisha as well as friendly chitchat and this was when I realised that this was the beginning of a new friendship. This was my ideal life, working hard to achieve your dreams, and once in a while go out and have fun with your friends, well balanced. Waled had a different perspective of life, he didn't want me to hang out with my friends which I felt was wrong. Why should I end my friendships most of those are from way before I had met him just because he tells me too? That was wrong, I had a life and he couldn't just walk in to my life and isolate me like that. He would say that one doesn't need friends when they have family. Now to me that is a big joke and we would fight a lot because I would tell him to get serious, you can't always tell family certain things, like you can friends. I didn't see myself hanging out with my mother telling her about the problems with

Najia Rasool

this ' poor excuse of a husband' I had now could I? He was a very jealous man and he always thought I was up to no good and that made me tick.

Well weeks went by and Vim and I kept in touch regularly. We decided to meet at the restaurant but it would be just myself and him as Naeeamah was working. It was good but I wasn't as relaxed because it felt like I was missing an arm or a leg without Naeemah there. I was surprised when Vim asked why she hadn't come with me because this was not something I was used to from Waled who never asked me how she was even though she had done so much for him when he had come to visit. Well the evening went well and we talked about what he planned to do after university and I planned to do in the future. Wow here was someone other than Naeemah who was actually interested in what I wanted to do, what I wanted to achieve. We continued to speak about family, work etc. The meal was not that good but we had become used to the rubbish service we received here but yet we still came back. After we finished the meal he walked me to my car, gave me a hug and said good-bye.

It was now end of October and life seemed the same, everyday seemed to get shorter and shorter, autumn was upon us. Work was boring because Naeemah had left and was now working for a coffee shop just a few shops away. She always came to see me when she was working, making sure to bring me a coffee and something small like cake, muffin, sandwich. We would come to work together on Sundays as we started around the same time and would have breakfast together at my work in the bar area. We took turns to bring cake, biscuits etc which we would share and drink tea with whilst chatting. After work we would wait for each other and go home together which was always good. When I was doing the late shift Naeemah would come see me after her shift and help me with a couple of things. She would wait until I closed the shop down so we would do the paper work together and then we would leave. Sometimes if she wasn't working she would call me when I was doing the paperwork and we would talk about what had happened that day and I enjoyed that. Naeemah told me about another job she had found that would be perfect for me as it didn't involve staying at work till the early hours of the morning and I was thrilled. We sat down and filled in all the forms one day when we were both off work. I was tired of doing the late shift and tired of not being able to progress any further than I was. I had already given my notice in to my manager a while ago when Waled had wanted to have the wedding in January. After Waled had changed his mind I had told my manager that I would be staying on for a little longer. After a few weeks we received an invitation for an interview. The interview was interesting and I did my best. After a while I received a letter informing me that I had a job providing I passed the security checks. Now I was sure that I wanted to leave because I didn't want to mess the manager around so I informed him that I would leave at the end of January. I knew that the checks would take a while so I decided to give myself sometime off before starting my new job. The last week at the shop was very hard as this was were I had worked for so long and I was at the top. I had made so many friends here and now I was closing this chapter of my life here.

I took the whole of February off whilst waiting for all the security checks to clear. I got a little bored at home and so Naeemah got me a job as a manager at the coffee shop where she worked. I was pleased because up till now I didn't know what was going on with the security checks and how long it would take. We were working together again and Naeemah taught me everything she knew about coffee. I made new friends and then I got transferred to another store in Windsor. This store was new and the manager took me under her wing which was good. After a month I received a letter in the post informing me that the training day for my new job at the airport would be in a few weeks. I was pleased but at the same time I was also confused as I had now started this new job at the coffee shop and thoroughly enjoyed it. I was achieving one of my dreams of managing a coffee shop here and didn't want to give it up but at the same time the other job had good career prospects. I decided that the best thing to do would be to work both jobs for a few weeks then make my decision because the last thing I wanted to do was to give up one job because the grass looked greener on the other side then later discover that I had made a big mistake. I went for training at the airport and the job was good but the coffee shop now seemed to much as the journey time was long and I would get so tired from trying to balance the two jobs that I decided to leave it and stay with my new job. I enjoyed the job as it was different and I had a great shift pattern.

Over the next couple of months I watched a few property programs about developing property in Dubai and I wished I could be one of those people who owned property in that beautiful country. I had felt so at home when I was there and the investment seemed worth it so I took a chance and began to try find more information on what purchasing a property involved. Naeemah and I looked around and found an agency not to far from my house who took me through different property options. I was a little scared as you were purchasing off plan. What if the property I would purchase turned out to be horrible? I looked at the brochures and went to other property exhibitions to see what they had to offer. After a few months of continuous work I decided that I needed a holiday to clear my head and relax before I made my decision on purchasing property in Dubai. Naeemah and I decided to go back to Dubai as we had had such a good time previously and this time we wanted to go to the Jumeriah beach Mosque and on a desert safari. Naeemah had just changed jobs and was now also working at the airport and so also agreed that we needed a holiday because the busy rush of summer holiday had tired her out. We booked our holidays and then counted down the days until we were in paradise again. We also decided that the best thing to do was to have a look at the area that the estate agents had offered me.

This time we took a direct flight to Abu Dhabi then took a coach to Dubai. When we arrived at the coach stop we noticed an estate agents and took down the number as we wanted to see if they had anything to offer us. We arrived at our hotel which was different to the hotel we had previously stayed at but it was on Jumeriah beach and it was beautiful. We were tired and so decided to take a nap and relax a bit. When we got up we took a walk and explored the hotel which was beautiful except the fact that there were building works going on right behind it. The gardens were beautiful, filled with green grass, flowers and water features that made the garden feel so surreal especially with the chirping birds in the palm trees. We explored the beach which was slightly smaller than the other beach we had been too but it was as beautiful. We enjoyed the rest of the day relaxing by the beach and in the gardens then made sure we took loads of pictures of the gardens in the evening when all the lights had been switched on. We went back to the room and changed then went out for dinner at the pool restaurant which was out in the open. It was very humid but we loved it. We had kofta kebabs and then shared a desert which was fantastic finishing off with some shisha and tea. We talked about what we would do the next day and that we had a lot to explore in the property developing issue.

After a good nights sleep we arose feeling fresh and ready for what the day had install for us. We got ready then went down to have break-fast which was excellent then caught a taxi to see this area where I was so close to purchasing a property. Something in my gut told me that I needed to have a look at this place because I was not convinced that it was going to be a beautiful place. The taxi driver drove us to the area, some parts were completed and had people living there whilst other areas where still under construction. The area it self didn't win me over and when I looked at the apartments there I knew that there was no way I could invest in this. The roads where very narrow and the apartments were not as they appeared in the brochures. Naeemah up till now had been positive that we would see the area and like it but when she saw this she quickly changed her mind. We were glad that we had taken the time to come out here and look at this development before making any life changing decisions. The taxi driver drove us straight to the Mazaya centre where we had an appointment with the estate agents. The office was so beautiful furnished with a water feature giving a relaxed calm feeling to anyone who was as anxious as I was. We waited to see a gentleman called Nassir and he talked to us about what he could offer me for the amount of money I had. He was a very good salesman but I was equally a good customer, making sure to ask as many questions. He was generally a very nice gentleman and he wanted to find something suitable for me. I wanted to see what the houses would look like but because I was buying offplan he decided to take us to other developments that had been completed that were similar to what he had in mind for me to purchase. Nassir took us to many different areas and gave us loads of information regarding purchasing property before dropping us off at our hotel. In our room we sat there and read over the information we had received then talked about the prospects of having a house here. We discussed the advantages, disadvantages as well as what this development would be good for. The idea was so over whelming and seemed challenging but the benefits seemed to draw me closer. I had to admit that this deal seemed better than what I had been offered at home. That night we got ready and went out to a very exclusive restaurant that was known for its celebrity association. When we got there everyone was looking at us probably because they thought we were celebrities or some rich man's daughters. We ordered and the meal was brought out in style which added to the buzz. We thoroughly enjoyed our meal and glanced over at the table next to us only to see Giorgio Armani having dinner with three Arab gentlemen. At first we didn't recognise him but when we did we just continued on as normal. The only disadvantage to this restaurant was that they didn't serve shisha so instead we had dessert and tea.

The next morning we returned to Nassir's office and talked some more before deciding to go ahead with the sale. I sat there with sweaty palms wonder if I was doing the right thing or not. Naeemah was as nervous as I was as she also knew that this was a life changing event. I signed the papers and got the ball rolling by paying the deposit. Everything went well and when we left the office I knew that I would have to work very hard to achieve this dream. When we got back to the hotel we relaxed and enjoyed the last day by going to the beach and relaxing. We enjoyed the beach and then went back to the room to get changed for dinner. We went to the beach restaurant which served us a really good meal of rice with lamb stew, salad and hot nan bread. We made room for our favourite desert Um Ali and tea before going for a walk to discuss what we had just done. We went back to the room and began packing our bags ready to leave the next day. This trip had been more business orientated than the first trip.

When I got back to London I had the pressure of my actions in Dubai on my shoulders as I had to send over my first instalment. Things were hard as the rate was low and I found I had to pay a lot more to make up the money in Dirhams. I was frustrated and began to think I had made a huge mistake. I knew I had to work hard in order to get the mortgage from the Dubai bank. It was towards the end of September so I knew I only had a few months before I would have to pay the next instalment, plus I had my wedding in November. Mum was proud of me and believed in me which made me feel so good. I didn't tell Waled for a while until one day when Leila called and taunted me about cancelling my wedding. She made fun of my dream of buying a house in Dubai and I snapped and told her, 'actually I did that three months ago'. There was silence on the other side and I knew I had to tell Waled before she got the satisfaction of doing it. I asked her not to tell him as I would do it myself. He was upset and told me I had to sell it but I refused and told him that if my Mum didn't have a problem with it then why should he? He calmed down but made it clear that he wasn't happy with it. I didn't listen to him because as far as I was concerned I was achieving one of my dreams. I continued to work hard and tried to save what I could.

One day I got an email from Emirates Airlines inviting me for an interview for Cabin Crew. I was so surprised as I hadn't applied for any vacancies but had only told Naeemah that Cabin Crew had been my dream job since that first flight as a child. Naeemah admitted she was behind this and I gave her a big hug. She told me that she didn't ask me because she knew I would come up with yet another excuse and that she wanted me to live life with no regrets. That was the most sweetest thing anyone has ever said to me and I appreciated her so much. There were so many people there that I didn't believe I would get anywhere but I decided to give it my best shot. I went for the first interview and got through to the next stage where I had to take a test. I was so worried I would fail the test but as usual Naeemah was there encouraging me to not give up. I was successful and was invited to the final stage which was a one on one interview. I was nervous and changed my outfit three times as I wanted to be perfect. The interview was good but I remained open minded as anything could happen. The only person who knew about this was Naeemah and mum. I would have to wait a few weeks before I would know if I got the vacancy or not. I went back to my usual life and almost forgot about it as I was busy trying to plan my holidays off to go to America for my wedding. It had been decided that the wedding would be on the last week-end of November. Leila, Waled's sister called to ask me to come over a month before the wedding so we could get everything ready together but I declined as I had a lot to do before then. Waled and his family wanted me to come over early and choose a wedding dress but I decided to leave that up to them to plan. I didn't really want to go there but knew I would have no choice. I didn't know how long I should stay there for as I had to be back as soon as possible to get ready to go to Dubai to sought out my mortgage. When I told Waled this he was furious and demanded I sell the house right away. I decided not to and then took time off work for the wedding. I would leave here two days before the wedding and come back before Christmas as no one could have Christmas off on leave at work. I ran this idea past mum and she disagreed as she thought it would not be right for us to leave just before Christmas so I negotiated at work to get more time off. I managed to get the time off but was not happy at having to be away for so long. Mum began to pack everything and get ready. My brother-in-law Yacob and Naeemah would accompany us to America to attend the wedding. I felt relieved that at least Naeemah would be there so I would have someone to talk to. The day before we were to depart I went shopping and asked Naeemah to come with me as I needed to get a few things. It was tradition that the bride wore green clothes which symbolised Islam. I couldn't find anything until I tried a shop in Brent Cross which had the perfect outfit. After we finished Naeemah came over and brought over a few things for me to pack into one of the suitcases then we put all the bags into the car and she left. Mum and I cleaned the house and threw everything out of the fridge as it would have gone off by the time we got back. I had a warm bath and as I sat there I pinch myself as I couldn't believe this was happening. Here I was going to America for my wedding in a few days. I had mixed feelings, with part of me happy and the other sad and upset. I went to bed and couldn't get to sleep despite how tired I was. My mind was racing with thoughts of 'my Wedding', it all seemed like I was dreaming.

The next morning was hectic as we all prepared to leave. Naeemah came over to pick up the rest of the luggage then went to the airport ahead of us to drop it off. She then went home and got changed as we were going to meet at the airport. Yacob came over to our house and we set off together. We had all checked in the night before so we went straight through to the departures area. Mum and Yacob went to the gate whilst Naeemah and I went around the perfume shops. I wanted to get my make-up done by this make-up artist I had heard about. After we had finished we went straight to the gate as boarding had commenced and when we got there we realised the we had been upgraded a class which made my day. I looked out the window and said good-bye to the country I had known as home because this young girl would come back a woman. The flight was good and I talked a lot, I guess to try and hide my fear. This was it, no turning back now. As we made our final approach my heart raced and I felt like I was dreaming and any minute now I would wake up at home in my normal life. I pinched myself and realised that this was as real as it could get. It took a while to taxi to the terminal building and then we all disembarked into this high lift bus. It was clearly unpleasant to be squashed in this bus thing and when we got to the terminal the immigration queue was very long. It was very different to our well organised immigration queues at home and we waited a long time. Whilst standing there I watched at how rude the immigration officers were handling some passengers. Why did they have to do that? After we collected our bags we walked out and I felt excited but anxious so I squeezed Naeemah's hand. I had told Waled not to come to the airport as I was upset with him. I was relieved to see that he was not there and instead I saw my sister Yasmeen who I had not seen for a number of years. She hugged us all and helped us with our bags to the cars where my cousin and his son waited for us. The drive home took a while and I couldn't believe how much woodland we drove through and how dark the city was compared to London. This was the capital of 'the super power,' I couldn't believe it. We were received into a home full of relatives I hadn't seen since my Kandahar days and others I had never seen before. Everyone was so excited to see us and some cried tears of joy. We sat down on the floor Afghani style and everyone talked and then Yasmeen left to go pick up Samir who was arriving shortly. They were all so happy that we had arrived safely and that Naeemah had travelled so far just to be there for me.

This made everyone realise how close we were and they treated Naeemah as I had she was my sister, my family. I felt so shy because everyone was looking at me, I was the centre of attention and that made me a little uneasy. Everyone began to talk to the people sitting next to each other giving me a chance to squeeze Naeemah's hand and she gave me what I needed, a smile full of love and reassurance then we engaged in conversation with our cousins around us. Dinner had been prepared and there was so was so many different types of food prepared, rice, salads, chicken, lamb just to mention a few which was all laid out in the centre of the circle. Just then the door bell rang and in came Yasmeen followed by Samir and everyone got to their feet. I couldn't believe my eyes, there she was, Samir just as I remembered her only older. She greeted everyone then came over and gave Naeemah and I each a big hug. I could see tears of happiness in everyone's eyes. I had told her so much about Naeemah that she felt that she knew her so well even though this was the first time they had actually meet and Naeemah too also felt like she had known Samir for ever. Everyone talked and we ate dinner then helped clear dishes away after everyone was finished, talking while doing everything. I felt tired because of the time difference and the days leading up to the journey had tired me out. Another factor that really made me upset was having to try deal with all the family pressure on my shoulders, at the airport no one from Waled's side had come to meet us and this made me feel upset not because I wanted them to but because my family wanted them to. I had told him not to be there as I was angry with him but I expected him to know that I didn't want him there but the rest of the family did and that was what was important. We finally retired and went upstairs to the room we were to sleep in. We were going to sleep in the same room as Samia, Yasmeen, and a couple of cousins and mum would sleep downstairs with other relatives. We didn't get straight to sleep as everyone was so busy talking and laughing but we eventually drifted off to sleep.

The next morning we woke up still feeling a little tired but we had to get up and help prepare breakfast. We sat down to have breakfast and everyone talked and laughed. Waled called to see how I was and then he spoke to mum. He came over a few hours later to see everyone and to pick up all my stuff to take them to his house. I spent the rest of the day just at home with my family then later on that afternoon I started getting ready for the Henna night which was a pre-wedding event. I changed and began to do my make-up but Yasmeen insisted on doing it for me and because I didn't want to upset her I agreed. She did my make up very different to how I liked it but I didn't complain I just let her get on with it and when she was done I thanked her. The whole family was so happy that I just played along, but inside I kept telling myself - ' oohh be happy, you can do this, just smile and act!' Everyone got ready and then the grooms party arrived and we all greeted them in the lounge area. Waled was wearing a suit and was given a traditional suit to change into then had to come sit next to me. After everyone gathered in the lounge we sat down and everyone was served tea and traditional snacks. Pictures were taken then everyone got up and we all got into vehicles that would take us to Waled's house where the Henna night would be held. Waled and I were driven by his brother, mum and Yacob sat in the car with us whilst Naeemah went with Leila. The drive was long and when I looked out the window all I could see was trees. This place had no street light as we did in London. When we finally arrived we were met by the rest of his family and then we proceeded down stairs where everything was set up in the basement. There were cushions on the floor for all the guests and a couch dressed in green material for Waled and I. Everyone talked and took pictures of us whilst some danced to the traditional Afghan music that played. We were then all invited upstairs to have dinner which was all laid out on the dinning table, from salad to kebabs to rice. Everyone sat down upstairs and helped themselves to some dinner and talked to other guests. After dinner we returned downstairs and pictures were taken and we all danced. Tea was served then Waled and I had to read a passage from the Koran and recite some prayers. After this followed the traditional henna ritual which involves putting henna in the palms of the ladies and on the pinkie finger of the young men. Everyone celebrated and had a good time dancing. It was great to see everyone having a good time even though I would have rather been else where. When the evening came to an end everyone said their good-byes to us then Waled's brother took Samia, Naeemah and my cousins home. Waled took mum, Yasmeen and myself home in his car and on the way home he told me he would come over the next day to take me to the hotel where the reception was to be held so that I could see it. Maybe I just felt like I was dreaming or perhaps I was so tired that I just gave him a nod. We arrived at home and everyone couldn't stop talking about how much they had enjoyed themselves. I went upstairs and got ready for bed then went and talked to Naeemah for a bit. Everyone went to bed as we were all very tired.

The next morning I woke up and just lay there for a while wondering how I got here and if this was what I was supposed to do. Everyone else started to get up and so I decided to do the same. Breakfast was served and everyone sat there after breakfast and talked. The mood was a little dull in the room because although the wedding was tomorrow evening we were thinking of how it would have been nice if Dad was still here with us. I felt sad and wondered if I would be here if he was still with us, or rather that I wouldn't mind being here if he was with us. We wiped the tears that streamed down our checks away and began to get ready for what the day had in-store for us. Waled came over at about noon and took me to the hotel to see how the reception area was prepared. On the way there we spoke about why he hadn't come to the airport, this discussion later became an argument. We stopped off to have some lunch at this Italian restaurant as Waled was hungry. I could tell he was upset but that didn't bother me as I was just as upset. After lunch we went to the hotel which was beautiful, surrounded by trees and gardens. Unfortunately the receptionist in the lobby informed us that the manager who had the key for the hall where our reception was to be held was not there and so we wouldn't be able to see it, so instead we walked around the rest of the hotel. Waled then took me home and told me he would see me later. When I got home everyone but my cousin Kareema had gone out to the local shopping mall so I helped her with the cooking and with her children until everyone came home. Naeemah and Samia had bonded very well and that made me happy as I knew that at least Naeemah wouldn't get bored quickly. Naeemah was very quiet though, I guess because she couldn't read how I fell or because she didn't know what she could do to make everything okay. It was nice to have my family here with me even though all of them couldn't be here. My sisters and I went upstairs to start making little traditional Afghan gift bags to give to the guests at the wedding the next day. Samia was cutting the cutting the green lace material into squares whilst Naeemah and I filled them with chocolate and Noqal and made little bows with the ribbon Samia had cut up. We talk whilst working and then Yasmeen came to join us. We had made quite a few by this time and then Yasmeen criticised the way Samia was cutting the material. All hell broke out and Samia got very upset and threw everything on the ground and stormed off while Yasmeen tried to tell her that she knew better. I immediately got up and ran after Samia, I couldn't stand to see her upset. I calmed her down and reminded her that Yasmeen was our sister and that that was the way she was. Samia calmed down and saw my point, we then returned to see that Naeemah had also spoken to Yasmeen who had then returned downstairs to be with mum. We finally finished and then went down stairs to join everyone else. We had dinner and helped clean up the house. More guests arrived for the wedding the next day and so we made tea for them and arranged the sleeping arrangements for everyone.

The next morning was hectic as everyone was busy thinking about what they would wear. I couldn't believe that this day had come, all this time I had done my best to not think about it but now I couldn't do anything but think about it. I had breakfast then Leila called to say that she had arranged for my hair and make-up to be done by a professional at the hotel. I was to be picked up by Waled who would drop me off and I would stay there and get dressed there too. Waled came to the house to pick me and Samia up and took us to the hair dresser who did my hair. Leila and her cousins were there when we arrived. The hair-dresser was nice and gave me a catalogue to look at different styles but unfortunately I didn't like the way she had done it as the finished product looked nothing like it was supposed to and so I had to instruct her what to do. She finally got it after I explained several times. After we were finished waled took us to the hotel where they had reserved 2 rooms for me and Waled to get ready. The make-up artist came to do my make-up. Samia got ready and then helped me into my wedding gown which was gorgeous. Looking into the mirror I couldn't believe that that was me and that this day had come. A few last minute adjustments were done and then it was time to go downstairs and join the guests.

We met Waled downstairs and then we walked together, hand in hand, side by side into the wedding reception where everyone was waiting for us. There were so many people there and as I walked in everyone was looking at us. We walked to the couch that had been traditionally decorated, then we stood there and the cameraman took loads of pictures. The musician Ahmed Wali was singing traditional Afghani songs and everyone started dancing and clapping for us. We took loads of pictures with different family members. Everyone sat down then we enjoyed the music. Guests got up and danced then we had to join them which was so embarrassing as all eyes were on us. We were then served dinner and there was so much food to choose from. There were so many deserts to choose from too from fresh fruit to Afghani traditional desert and noqal. Tea was served to everyone and when everyone was full they danced. The reception hall was well decorated with tables and chairs around the dance floor. We took more photos and then we had to sit and watch the guests dancing. After a while we had to perform some traditional rituals that involved covering us with a shawl and giving us a mirror to see each others faces in. We then had to feed each other a tiny bit of salt, chocolate, and traditional desert. I then had to hold a glass of juice to Waled's mouth for him to drink and vice versa and this was followed by reciting verses from the Qu'ran. We then had to cut our wedding cake and feed it to each other then it was cut up and served to all the guests. Celebrations continued into the night until about one in the morning when we started saying good-bye to guest. The last photos were done with both families and when everyone left we went up to the hotel room where we were going to spend our first night.

The next morning we got up and got ready then left and passed by to see my family as this was tradition. We had breakfast with the family and then left to go to his home. We sat with his family, talked and then got ready for the arrival of my family in the evening so we could complete the tradition with the final ceremony. They arrived and everyone had dinner and we went downstairs where all the gifts were unveiled. I received loads of gold, money and other gifts from everyone. The celebrations continued and everyone had a good time, dancing and taking photos of us. The night eventually came to an end and everyone went home. Here I was in their house, with their son - my husband. I had always felt like things would work themselves out, that once I was here with him I everything would fall into place but here I was still feeling the same way I had felt when I first got engaged. Had I made a mistake? Was I going to feel this way for the rest of my life with him?

I continued to play the happy bride but deep down I wanted to go home and continue living my life as it was before all this. I wanted to be with my mum and the rest of my family. The next day Yasmeen left to go home and it was very sad for me and everyone else. This was a reality check for me because up till now it hadn't hit home that everyone would be leaving soon including Samia and Naeemah leaving mum and I here with these people. I dreaded the days that followed and didn't want to think about them. I briefly saw Naeemah and Samir that day as they were taken out to see Washington DC and when they return in the evening Waled came to pick me up. The next day Naeemah was due to leave and that afternoon we went over to have lunch with them. We spoke, laughed and despite my best efforts to try suppress my feelings. I gave in and my eyes watered up and the tears ran down my checks. How was I going to survive here without my 'right hand-man'. I felt lost, alone, angry and disappointed because everything hadn't worked out the way I had wanted it to. Naeemah and I had been inseparable and now we were to live apart for a whole month and just the thought of that made me feel alone.

The days dragged on and I felt like my spirit was dying, but still there was a glimmer of hope. I counted the days as they passed and knew I was getting closer to going home. Waled's and his family wanted me to stay on but I was lucky because I had to go home and sought out my visa in order to live and work there. Every time the phone rang and it was Naeemah, my spirits would lift and I would feel happy. I was going to be a good wife, daughter-in-law, sister-in-law as not to disappoint my family. The whole family was really nice to me and this made life easier. Every morning I would get up and make breakfast for everyone and then quickly clean the house. We would spend most of the time at home and some evenings we would either go out or have guests over. This was not like other couples who would go on their honey moon then enjoy their married life together. After a couple of weeks it was time to go home and everyone was very upset that I had to leave.

As soon as the aircraft doors opened and we walked off the aircraft into London Heathrow I felt my heart jump up and down. I was glad to be home even though the weather was horrible. Naeemah was there to meet us and mum and I gave her a big hug, anyone who didn't know us would think that we hadn't seen each other for years. After a few days back things went back to the way they were before I went to America, I started working hard again because I had to sought out the mortgage in Dubai. The whole of January I worked hard so that Naeemah and I could go to Dubai in February. Everything was arranged for the trip and we then decided that spending a week there was going to be enough. Unfortunately when we got there things didn't go the way we had hoped. Everything was moving at a snails pace and we spent most of our time chasing people to try get things done but it was like pushing a train with its brakes on. The weather was horrible to, constantly raining which made the holiday very boring. Everyday we kept hoping things would fall into place but it wasn't meant to be. I must admit this was a very stressful time of my life and I was so close to throwing it all away. Even Naeemah was stressed and even though she tried to remain positive for me I could see that she was beginning to think that things were going pear-shaped but didn't want me to give up hope as that was all we had. After our brief stay it was time to go home, disappointed that things hadn't gone according to plan. I would have to go home and work very hard for the next couple of months before coming back and giving this the last shot. Coming home without succeeding was hard and it made me feel a bit depressed but I knew that I had to do this.

As soon as I got back I arranged to work extra shifts and it took a while to adjust. I would get so tired and sometimes I would almost loose all hope that everything would go well but I had encouragement from mum and Naeemah who supported me. Armed with everything I needed we started faxing documents over to the bank manager in Dubai and whilst I worked Naeemah liased with them to arrange our next trip when everyone would be present for us to get everything done. The trip was planned and we got ready for it too. I was not convinced that everything would go according to plan and I felt certain that I would loose the house. I was prepared to fight for it because it meant a lot to me. When we arrived the weather was lovely and we settle into our hotel room well. We went off to see the bank manager and he briefed us on what was going to happen and the whole process. It sounded so straight forward but I knew that it was probably not going to be so simple. After a few days we still heard nothing and this really made my spirits sink as I could see myself loosing the house. We thought that everything would be completed by day four as we had planned to go to Abu Dhabi for a few days. We were in a predicament as if we went to Abu Dhabi things may start to move and we would have to drive all the way back and if we remained in Dubai we would miss our trip to Abu Dhabi. I was loosing hope as things weren't going according to plan. Was this going to turn out the way I planned or was everything going to fall apart? I wasn't enjoying this at all because I was someone who liked to be in control. Everyday we would wait for a call from the bank manager but nothing happened. I was annoyed because we were letting this dominate our holiday and this didn't give us a chance to see Abu Dhabi. Some mornings we would go have break-fast, come back and sit in our room watching TV, reading the paper or sleeping. Sometimes we would go out but only to the shopping centres as we couldn't afford spending too much money. In the evening we would have dinner and go to our room and watch TV. One evening we went out with only 15 Dirhams in our purse and of course there was no place that sold anything that cheap until we came across this Lebanese restaurant equivalent to our break-fast café at home. This place had cheap kebabs for 5 Dirhams and we each got one and returned to the hotel room. We were both so hungry that we ate very quickly and when we were done I had to express my opinion about the food. I guess we were both tense and sometimes we would argue about silly things and then make amends because we needed one another. After three days we had to leave and continue our 'tour'. We drove to another Emirate state Ras al Khaimah which was about two hours away and when we got there we were tired. The hotel we stayed in was not that great but I guess the fact that my friend Mary and her boyfriend Mike was staying there made up for it. We had the buffet dinner which was very nice and after that we met up with them for a shisha and tea. They were so happy to see us and we talked so much, for a while I forgot about everything going on. The next day we drove to Dubai to see the manager as my strategy was to put pressure on them so something would happen but nothing happened. We went out for dinner with Mary and Mike and they managed to lift our spirits. We laughed and joked and so by the end of the night we felt so much better. The next day we returned to Dubai and spent the day in the car just parked on the side of the road outside a shopping mall not knowing what we were doing. As the sun finally set we decided that we had to make last minute arrangements for a hotel room because we had to increase our days in Dubai. The bank manager was now sounding a little more positive and reassured us that things were going to start moving. I wasn't too sure but I kept hoping he was right. We booked a night at one of our favourite hotels and settled in nicely. We relaxed by the roof-top swimming pool which was very quiet. The view was beautiful and I said a prayer that everything would fall into place. We had dinner at Nando's that night which was really nice and then relaxed for the rest of the evening. The next day we were awoken at about seven by a text message from the bank manager informing me that he had good news, his manager had approved the mortgage and now we just had to wait for the document to be printed. We got up and had break-fast and then rang the manager but there was no reply. We went to our usual day area, the roof-top pool where we relaxed and talked. We rang him but there was no answer, which made me feel like breaking down in tears because I needed reassurance that everything was going to turn out well. We waited for some sought of news and I decided to further extend our stay. Time was now running out because we only had 2 more days before Naeemah had to be back at work and I had to ring work to tell them I had to extend my holiday.

The next morning we got up and went to have breakfast when we received a call that everything was ready and that I had to come and sign the papers and get everything signed off. My heart jumped and I just couldn't wait to get everything done and leave. We had break-fast quickly and packed our stuff away before settling the bill and driving to the bank as fast as possible. When we got there we gave the manager a big smile and thanked him for all his hard work. The bank manager kept smiling telling me to prepare myself as I had to sign 'only 49times!'. I was surprised at how many times I had to sign the mortgage document because I thought he was just joking but it turned out he wasn't. Once we finished signing everything I was so happy I felt like screaming. Naeemah was still in shock and just gave me a big hug. We had been through so much and now it was finally drawn to a close. We thanked everyone for all their hard work and left for the airport as we had to make the afternoon flight to London. I didn't want to spend anymore time here after this ordeal, well not at that time. We got to the airport and checked in and when we sat in our seats my held hands and congratulated each other. I was on top of the moon and said a little prayer to Allah for never leaving my side and making all this possible.

I returned to work a happy woman and I now have a new out-look on life. Sometime things happen for a reason and other times when one door closes another opens. You can achieve anything you want to, if you put your mind and your heart to it with the support of family and friends you can accomplish any dream no matter how big it is. At certain stages of one's life you can feel alone even though you are surrounded by family and friends but with Allah anything is possible.

Glossary

Imam- Leader of Muslim congregation.

Nikah- Muslim wedding.

Qu'ran- Muslim Holy Book

Noqal -sugared almonds